W9-CDF-122

How to Get MILLION DOLLAR GIFTS *and Have Donors* Thank You!

How to Get MILLION DOLLAR GIFTS and Have Donors Thank You!

Robert F. Hartsook, JD, EdD

ASR Philanthropic Publishing

Wichita, Kansas

Additional copies of this book are available from the publisher. Discounts may apply to large-quantity orders.

Address all inquiries to:
ASR Philanthropic Publishing
P.O. Box 782648
Wichita, Kansas 67278
Telephone: 316.733.7470
Facsimile: 316.733.7103

Designed by Roger Keating, Mennonite Press, Newton, Kansas.
Back cover photograph by Denny Collins, Phoenix, Arizona.
Printed in the United States of America by Mennonite Press, Newton, Kansas.

ISBN: 0-9663673-1-6

Library of Congress Catalog Card Number: 99-072588

Publisher's Cataloging-in-Publication
(Provided by Quality Books, Inc.)

Hartsook, Robert F.
    How to get million dollar gifts and have donors
    thank you / Robert F. Hartsook. — 1st ed.
    p. cm.
    Includes bibliographical references.
    ISBN: 0-9663673-1-6

    1. Fund raising. 2. Charitable uses, trusts,
    and foundations. 3. Nonprofit organizations—Finance.
    I. Title.

HV41.2.H37 1999   361.7068'1
                      QBI99-478

Contents

Integrity: Do What You Say You'll Do

Putting the Gift Together

Thank You... Thank You... And by the Way, Thank You!

Demonstrating the Gift's Impact— Making a Difference

Fund Raiser, Let's Get Personal

Nobody Else Will Unless You Do!

Acknowledgments

Remembering 101 fund-raising stories is a daunting task. Obviously, these strategies are the result of decades of experience. Reviewing each, testing each and presenting each confidentially has also proven to be a significant undertaking for me, my editors and colleagues.

The individuals who inspired these stories are too many to mention. I appreciate their willingness to talk to me and share their experiences.

Fund-raising professionals have added significantly to this work through their insight and observations. I am grateful to those in the profession who continue to make personal fund raising a powerful tool.

Technically, this book is the result of many hours of work by Denise Rhoades, Linda Cruse, Annette Lough, Stan Thiessen, Susan Sellers, and Jennifer Buchanan. Shelly Chinberg, who has served as my assistant for more than a decade and heard most of these stories firsthand, has been vital in correcting my memory. My sincere thanks to each for their tireless efforts.

Finally, I am continually grateful to my mentor and friend, Art Frantzreb.

Bob Hartsook

Foreword

Inspiring people to make significant gifts is an obsession I have had my entire career. Every time a new project confronts me, I begin looking for the donor nobody knows about and how that donor could make a million-dollar gift. Over the years, my donors have frequently become philanthropic celebrities in their communities.

Sometimes a few donors receive the lion's share of publicity. I value their gifts, but I don't expect them to consider all causes equally. So, unearthing a donor nobody knows about gives me wonderful satisfaction.

Most philanthropists do not seek celebrity status. Many are mentioned in this book, and they are referred to either by real or fictitious first names. Once, a major donor to a university that I served told me that he never wanted to see or hear of his name on any prospect list. So, the Director of Development, Murray Blackwelder (now vice president of Iowa State University), and I came up with the alias *Seymour*. His code name was on every list. This prospect, while participating in donor screening meetings, would come across the name *Seymour* and ask, "Who is this?" We would say that "Seymour" was from out of town.

Seymour is just one of many philanthropists I have met. I love them for their philanthropy, and this book is devoted to celebrating their good work. I am proud of the character of the men and women philanthropists whose stories I tell in this volume. Wealth is not their success; it only leads to their success.

Finally, I want to say a word to my fellow fund raisers. We are a curious lot. Philanthropy needs fund raisers committed to raising funds and doing it well. I hope this book highlights the qualities of good fund raising by professionals or volunteers.

If you like our strategies and land a million-dollar donor, congratulations! Write and tell me your story. Maybe you will find yourself on the pages of the next book.

Bob Hartsook

Dedication

To Austin, my son and best friend.

How to Use This Book

You don't have to sit down and read this book cover to cover. In fact, that is probably the wrong thing to do. These 101 strategies have come from real life experiences. While I have protected the confidentiality of each of these donors and institutions, everything in this book really happened.

First, you must decide whether your agency or institution could use a million-dollar or more gift. You think that is an easy question, but it's not. For over a year I have asked audiences that question. Most say yes: some don't. If you don't think your institution could use a million-dollar gift, then don't read this book.

Second, remember my number one philosophical tenet: "Nobody wants to give money away." Don't ever forget it, but remember number two is: "They will give to change people's lives."

Third, have you realized that most wealth in America is held by individuals, and that your best chance to receive gifts is from an individual, not a corporation or a foundation.

Fourth, do you know that your gift is probably going to come from a prospect who isn't on everyone else's prospect list? Your best opportunity comes from your prospect, not someone else's.

Fifth, does hard work bother you?

Well, now you're ready. Look over the table of contents. The strategies are organized loosely, but you may want to sample some from the front, middle, and back. Try the titles that intrigue you. Eventually read them all.

Marguerite, a donor friend of mine, responded to my invitation for her to come to an organizational meeting of a campaign, "I'll come because I think I'm going to learn something." Read along. I think you'll learn something. Marguerite thanked me for inviting her.

Opportunity Is Always Present

Listen, Listen, Listen

The Principle

Show respect for the donor by asking questions that invite her to share her ideas, principles and values. A good question, such as, "How did you become successful?" can give rise to yet other valuable questions. Through such conversations, each donor is able to talk about what he finds important, troubling, inspiring or intolerable. Such information is a gold mine for a fund raiser. By recognizing the donor's successes and actively listening, a fund raiser learns about the donor's life, family and values.

The Story

A donor named Evan shared that the most important thing he learned in college was how to communicate effectively. Marguerite, believed her financial success was due to her ability to relate well to people. Warren shared that the premature death of two children had given him a deep appreciation of life. Wilma explained that while her husband was alive she had paid close attention to their business so that when he died, she knew the operation. Richard revealed that during the twenty years he has been in business he has always had a six-month crisis plan.

Through such conversations, a fund raiser learns about family frailties, relational problems and other important issues. Every aspect of life—failures, setbacks and successes—will be discussed over time if a fund raiser genuinely values a donor as both a person and not simply as a source of money. Evan and Marguerite both ultimately made gifts of more than $1 million.

The Lesson

A fund raiser who listens to a donor will be listened to by the donor. A fund raiser who truly values a donor will be valued in return.

Go Where Others Haven't

The Principle

"Go West!" was the advice commonly offered 150 years ago. Many heeded this advice. Some people, while not heading west themselves, participated in this opportunity by supplying the goods and services needed by those who were heading west.

Sam Walton, icon of unconventional business wisdom, found opportunities in retail sales by swimming upstream. When the gold rush in retail sales was attracting most major retailers to urban areas, Walton's big, blue-striped buildings began appearing in smaller communities. He achieved success, not by following his competitors, but by looking elsewhere. He earned a permanent place in retail history by serving people who had previously been overlooked.

The Story

Several years ago when an older theater in a mid-sized city needed rehabilitation, an energetic organization decided to raise the necessary funds—several million dollars.

The organization began by reviewing its list of subscribers, members and annual donors, hoping to solicit commitments from those who had shown a long-standing interest in the theater. They received a few large donations, but then the gift-giving stalled. Although they had followed a normal course for fund raising, their goal eluded them.

With a consultant's guidance they began to look for other possibilities. First, they considered who attended the theater and why. Creating a composite profile of these individuals enabled the fund-raising organization to pinpoint a common denominator: the social aspect of theater events. People came early and stayed late, meeting friends before the event and unwinding from busy workdays. They exchanged the pressures of the day for the relaxing buzz of pleasant conversation. The anticipation of the evening was as much for the playful atmosphere of the theater as it was for the production event itself.

Theatergoers also often continued their evening at an area restaurant or at a reception honoring the cast, prolonging their theater experience well beyond the actual production.

After compiling this picture of theater users, the campaign group was challenged to look in the opposite direction. They then came up with a list of individuals who did not fit the standard profile of theater goers. This new group included people who came late and left early.

The campaign group identified ten such individuals. Of these, several were physicians who followed this different attendance pattern due to emergencies and other work responsibilities. Others attended not for their own enjoyment, but to accommodate their spouses.

In the list the campaign group discovered a gem.

Marion had enjoyed a long and close marriage with Jennifer who shared his love for the theater. They attended regularly, moving through the crowd of happy friends, mixing and chatting before the play began. They had lingered over many meals afterward, laughing, discussing the play, and enjoying one another.

However, for the ten years since Jennifer's death, Marion had been attending the theater alone. Although he still loved the performances, he could not confront the social aspect of the event. He found it easier to just slip in and out quietly.

Eventually, Marion made a $1 million gift to the campaign. This was a turning point in the fund-raising effort as well as for Marion personally. Marion's previous avoidance of the theater's social aspects gave way to his full social participation. He was grateful.

The Lesson

In every institution there are people who do not appear to fit. A childless person, for example, may give to a children's agency. Behind each situation is a unique individual story, a human story. The nature of this uniqueness may point to spectacular opportunities.

Rather than simply following well-worn fund-raising formats, a development professional must learn to view a situation from a fresh perspective.

Target The Big Gift Prospects

The Principle

The ultimate goal of a fund raiser is to meet the established financial project level, an amount targeted by the fund raiser and the institution or agency. This goal is generally ambitious, and achieving it requires specific strategies. Since attaining the financial goal is critical to the success of the agency and the fund raiser, it is beneficial to target "big gift" prospects. The amount that constitutes a "big gift" varies among agencies.

To get a big gift, you must first identify, research and cultivate those individuals who have the financial capability as well as sufficient interest in the cause to give a large amount.

The Story

Following the recommendations of a feasibility study, a hospital established a fund-raising goal of $50 million. A review of potential donors enabled the fund raisers to project that their largest gifts would probably be in the range of $2 to $3 million. Although they would solicit gifts of all amounts, the fund raisers believed the success of the fund drive would depend on the number of $100,000 to $1 million gifts received.

The fund raisers outlined and designed the campaign strategy knowing that most people do not give to hospitals in general. Instead, donors usually respond to a specific branch of medicine—heart research, cancer treatment, children's diseases. So, the campaign leadership established discipline-related campaign sub-committees responsible for developing prospects and solicitation strategies specific to certain areas of medicine.

The fund raisers focused first on donors who had the capability of giving $1 million or more. Next, they focused on donors who could give $100,000 or more. As the project unfolded, they received a lead gift of $1 million. The donor of this large initial gift, Bob, felt that his life had been saved by the work done through heart research and treatment. A subsequent solicitation resulted in an additional gift that increased Bob's total gift to $2.5 million. Bob was grateful to be alive to make this gift.

Another long-time donor, Zelda, although living in a different city, had always believed in the strength of this hospital's cancer treatment center; she donated $2 million. Zelda said that she had always wanted to make the gift, but was not convinced the hospital needed it. Harold, the director of development, emphasized that her gift was needed and valued. As Zelda reflected on her gift, she said, "I'm satisfied that this is the most effective place for me to give."

The agency also received several other $1 million gifts, eventually raising nearly $60 million. There were more than 100 gifts of $100,000 or more. The campaign finished without the fund raisers ever having to research prospects at the $50,000 level.

The fund raisers completed this successful campaign by focusing on major gift donors exceeding their campaign goal by $9 million.

The Lesson

While it is good to have a broad base of support at all levels, the bottom line frequently becomes, "Has the money been raised?" Critical to a fund raiser's ability to answer in the positive is whether big gift donors have been solicited.

Expect 99 percent of the funds raised to come from one percent of the donor base. Whether $1,000 or $1 million is perceived as a big gift, a large share of your fund-raising goal should consist of large gifts from major gift prospects. The old rule was that 80 percent of the funds raised came from 20 percent of the donors. Many examples in recent campaigns, however, suggest that the largest share of campaign donations comes from only one percent of the donors.

By thinking big, a fund raiser significantly decreases the time it takes to reach the agency's goal.

Persistence
Is
Rewarded

The Principle

Relationship building is not always easy. Many relationships are like flames that must be continually fanned. As with any effort, persistence in establishing relationships is often rewarded.

The Story

Stan had been the executive director of a youth program for many years. Although it was the extension of a national organization, Stan had served as the founder and leader of the local unit. Each day he worked hard to ensure that the organization was represented properly. He made every effort to see that the work was clearly noticed by those who had the resources to assist and advance its worthy cause.

Richard was a philanthropist who was known to support many institutions. Richard made the comment publicly that he wanted to be known as "The Philanthropist" of his state. Stan, eager to pursue Richard for a possible gift to the youth organization, began by inviting him to an event. Richard, who received many such invitations, sent a polite note of regret.

Finally, Stan was invited to an event at which Richard was being honored with an award. During the reception, Stan congratulated

Richard for receiving the award and was able to briefly mention the youth organization. He let Richard know that he had been trying for some time to get him to visit the facilities, but had failed. Richard said that he would stop by sometime. He did stop by and after several months of recognition, cultivation and involvement, Richard eventually gave $1 million to launch an effort for a youth recreation project.

The Lesson

As Richard was being publicly recognized for his gift to the youth project, he turned to Stan and said, "Thanks for your persistence!" In Stan's case, it paid off.

Success Lies In the Hands Of a Few

The Principle

Everyone who supports an agency or institution plays a role, but usually only a small percentage hold in their hands and heart the power to affect the destiny of an agency through giving. If a fund raiser identifies these people first, progress towards success accelerates.

Once these individuals are identified, they need to be empowered. Do not let these important people remain idle. Instead, advance their leadership positions, and let their voices be heard. Like a motor in a vehicle, these people do not represent the largest portion of an agency, but revved up, they can drive the agency toward its goals.

The Story

Murray had four daughters, each active in Girl Scouts. Having seen firsthand the importance of the organization, he enthusiastically joined the local Girl Scout board.

Murray accepted the position on the board, knowing that the traditional Girl Scout fund-raising activity was cookie sales. As a direct Girl Scout activity, however, cookie sales was going out of favor. Yet, the need for program support was continually increasing. Murray chose to view these sales as a special event rather than the main source of funding. He recognized the cookie sales as a signature special event, but an inadequate means of raising the funding necessary to support and advance the mission of the organization. Murray believed philanthropic efforts were essential.

During his tenure on the board of directors, Murray rose to the position of president. As president, he was able to influence others and demonstrate the importance of fund raising. Annual support increased, special events were financially more productive and his interest in large gifts gave the staff and volunteers a valuable new focus.

Murray came to believe that those individuals, corporations and foundations interested in youth-related programs would like Girl Scouting. He identified his friend and business associate, Terry, who was the head of a large family foundation, as a prospect who would care and could do something about it. Over time, Terry became interested in Murray's work. He saw the need for improved camp facilities and thought the Girl Scouts should try to secure a maintenance endowment for support of the camps. Other members of Terry's family agreed and eventually gave more than $1 million. His example advanced the Girl Scouts' philosophy and philanthropic efforts.

The Lesson

Terry would tell you that Murray "opened his eyes" to this important cause. He and his family are now deeply involved in providing regular leadership and financial support.

Look carefully for individuals who can be the driving force behind a fund-raising effort. These people—roughly 10 percent of those involved—can make a 100 percent difference in the outcome.

Create Asset Builders

The Principle

Fund raising is simply a means to an end and should never be an agency's primary focus. Each charitable board needs committed asset builders—individuals who have a sense of the long-range plans of the organization. The building of human assets becomes the power behind the fund raising. It is like the horse that pulls the fund-raising cart; money naturally follows. Service is the raison d'être of a nonprofit organization.

The Story

Jay was an asset builder who cared a great deal about a local hospice. He helped the hospice through a number of different volunteer capacities and gave modest financial gifts.

During a hospice meeting, Jay was challenged by what Norma, the executive director, had to say. Norma described what she considered to be the hospice's role in the community—an organization of significance, vitality and great worth. She discussed with the other board members the importance of their responsibilities, which reached far beyond merely voting on operational issues.

Norma challenged the board members to embrace the ambitious dreams and vision of the hospice project. The board responded with

100 percent participation, each making a "stretch" gift to the organization. The support of these board members gave Jay confidence that his funds would be well used and as a result of Norma's encouragement, Jay ultimately donated $3 million to the hospice project.

The Lesson

Asset building is more than acquiring dollars. Asset building means building human capital. A charitable board must be comprised of asset builders. These men and women must be willing to give their time, energy, talents and other resources to accomplish the goals and ambitions of the agency. Frequently, the money will follow.

Millionaires Are Investors

The Principle

New millionaires invest, on average, about 20 percent of their income annually. Fund raisers who are aware of this trend can use philanthropic tools as profitable long-term investments. Fund raisers need to be familiar with planned-gift strategies that provide innovative investment opportunities for donors.

The Story

Jill and Mark lived a very comfortable life. By the time they reached their late 50s, they had attained millionaire status. While they enjoyed their money, they were never ostentatious or flamboyant with their wealth. As the couple planned for the future, they anticipated their own needs, as well as those of their family. They began to invest some of their funds using various charitable instruments.

Mark wanted to establish an endowed chair at the school of medicine where he had completed his residency. Mark already had $3 million invested in a pension fund. He believed these proceeds would go into his estate upon his death and that his family would realize the funding. Mark was wrong. Mark's estate would have been taxed at a high level—as much as 85 percent. An informed fund raiser brought this to Mark's attention, and he decided he could meet his family's needs *and* give to his medical school. So, Mark withdrew $1.5 million of the $3 million pension fund, paid the taxes and penalties and bought a single-premium life insurance policy with designated family beneficiaries. As a result, Mark left $3 million to his family through his estate, met the legal requirements of his premature distribution of his pension and funded a chair at his medical school.

This creative thinking was the product of a resourceful fund raiser who, recognizing the donor's desire to give, developed an appropriate strategy.

The Lesson

Millionaires are going to invest. Mark and Jill are proud of their gift to the school and their family. Investing can be done efficiently and effectively through philanthropy, because philanthropy invests in people.

Most Children Of Millionaires Attend Private Schools

The Principle

Only 17 percent of today's millionaires attended private schools, yet 55 percent of their children and grandchildren do. Men and women who have worked hard and accumulated large sums of money clearly value a quality education.

Millionaires are in a financial position to affect the next generation, and most want their children and grandchildren to benefit from these more expensive educational opportunities.

The Story

Sylvester and Ellen developed a trash collection business together. The couple's business grew steadily and eventually became highly profitable. Neither Sylvester nor Ellen had ever attended college, and only Ellen had graduated from high school. However, the couple's three children all graduated from college.

Sylvester and Ellen's commitment to education extended to their grandchildren. Taking advantage of a tax loophole, the couple paid tuition at a private school for each of their grandchildren, who lived in a different community.

Ellen also supported a local charity. One day the charity's

development officer, Dave, remarked, "It is so nice that your children are able to educate your grandchildren at such a tremendous private school."

Ellen responded, "What do you mean, 'our children'? Sylvester and I are doing this ourselves!"

Dave realized that he had identified good prospective donors. As a result, he substantially increased the size of the gift he later requested from the couple and eventually received a gift of $2 million.

The Lesson

Review closely lists of parents and grandparents of children attending private educational institutions. These are individuals who are more concerned with the value of education than with the cost of tuition. This list is an excellent starting point for research and cultivation.

Don't Play Golf

The Principle

Choose cultivation activities carefully. While personal preferences may influence your choices, consider primarily the value of an activity in terms of cultivating relationships. Many believe that a good round of golf is the key to successful philanthropy. The truth is that thousands of fund raisers do their jobs extremely well without knowing a hook from a slice.

The Story

Jeff and Kevin were fund raisers within the same university. There was a subtle, yet long-standing sense of competition between the two. Despite their congenial rivalry, they enjoyed seeing one another succeed.

Kevin liked to play golf. He also felt that the game could play a significant role in developing relationships and securing large gifts. Jeff, on the other hand, was not a golfer. Jeff decided that there were better ways to enrich relationships than by playing golf poorly.

Kevin and Jeff made a deal. Kevin would play a round of golf with prospective donors while Jeff took the same amount of time, around four-and-a-half hours, to solicit donors. Afterward, they would compare scorecards.

For his round of golf, Kevin carefully selected his foursome. He invited a local banker who was on the verge of giving a significant gift. He chose a plant manager from a local manufacturing company, and to support his closing appeal, he included the president of the university.

For his time allotment, Jeff lined up seven half-hour appointments. His prospects included a retired school teacher who was interested in establishing a scholarship at the university, a businessman Jeff was just getting to know, the owner of a major franchise who was a big sports enthusiast, two local representatives of a national corporation, a faculty member who had been active in the university's phone campaign and another community prospect.

Kevin succeeded in closing both of his prospects at $100,000 and $300,000 respectively.

Jeff, on the other hand, collected an estate gift designation from the retired school teacher for $250,000. He received a commitment from the franchise owner for a $50,000 scholarship. From the faculty member, the university received $75,000, plus an inclusion in an insurance policy for $250,000. Jeff received gifts of $25,000 each from the two local corporate representatives and $100,000 each from two other appointments. In addition, he was able to develop a new relationship with the local businessman.

Although Kevin raised a substantial amount in his afternoon of golf, Jeff closed more gifts at a greater amount in the same time period.

The Lesson

Choose wisely. Create the best environment to achieve the greatest result. In fund raising, as in golf, the goal is to do the most with the least effort. Choose appropriately, and follow through. Then celebrate.

Look for The Childless Prospect

The Principle

In our society a growing number of couples over the age of 40 do not have children. This demographic is important in several ways. First, these individuals have more discretionary income. Additionally, without direct heirs, their estate-planning decisions are not as obvious. They represent some of the greatest prospects available to an agency.

Have you ever read a newspaper article about someone who died and left a large, unsolicited gift to an institution? If these stories were collected and studied, some common elements would inevitably emerge. Typically, the donors were over the age of 90 and made the gifts to universities or hospitals. Most were women without children. They often had some association with the institution in the distant past. The relationship may have been indirect—possibly even with someone associated with the organization, a person admired and trusted who showed care and concern.

The normal response of the receiving institution is, "We had no idea this gift was coming. We have never even heard of this individual." This is revealing. Why was this person never identified, befriended and given the chance to enjoy the recognition and impact of the gift?

Fund raisers who understand the human implications of these statistics should make every effort to discover and cultivate relationships with these unknown philanthropists.

The Story

As a young woman, Gretchen had attended a private school. She had gone to an exclusive private college and earned her master's degree from a major state university located in the city where she lived. She never married and had no children. She taught school for more than 40 years and had an enduring appreciation for the value of education.

Despite Gretchen's years of association with many prestigious institutions, she had never been cultivated or solicited for a gift. Why? Because she did not live in the "right" neighborhood. She never looked or acted as though she had great wealth. No one ever sought her out and questioned her about her love of learning. No one ever asked about her wealth of experience regarding education. She was overlooked and undervalued. As a result, her million-dollar gift did not go to the independent school, to the exclusive private college, or to the large university in her own city. Instead, Gretchen left a large gift—$1 million—to a local community college, affirming her belief both in education and humility. Gretchen's gift sent a strong message to the more prestigious schools she had attended.

The Lesson

Look for people who were active in or associated with the agency more than 30 years ago. Be especially sensitive to prospects without obvious heirs. Consider how they can play a strong and vital role in the institution. Do not let someone die without providing an opportunity for that person to be encouraged and energized by philanthropy. Remember those who do not have children. They may have devoted time and energy to another worthy avenue.

Exceed Donor Expectations

The Principle

Fund raising can be exhilarating, especially when donors' expectations are exceeded. However, it is not easy to exceed expectations. A fund raiser must first establish reasonable expectations then develop a strategy to go beyond them. Out-of-the-ordinary results are rarely achieved without a careful strategy.

In making a solicitation it is critical to be exceedingly clear about the donor's expectations. What will the donor's relationship be with the institution? What specific provisions of recognition, acknowledgment, affirmation and stewardship will follow the gift? Will a room or a building be named for the donor? What public form will the recognition take—a ceremony or a reception? What follow-up efforts are needed from the fund-raiser? Should donors expect a report detailing the use of their gifts or any other pertinent information?

When these expectations are not explicitly defined, everyone involved is set up for disappointment. Without clear explanations, a donor forms an impression from his own life experiences. These preconceived (but unsubstantiated) expectations can create big trouble for the fund raiser.

The Story

Marilee had given a substantial endowment gift to a university. In recognition, the university was to name an area of a new building in her honor. Organizers told her that a portrait would be commissioned and presented during a formal public announcement. Additionally, she could expect to receive annual reports on how the endowed funds were maintained and distributed.

In an effort to surpass Marilee's expectations, organizers crafted a thoughtful strategy. Before commissioning her portrait, organizers first determined what Marilee considered to be her favorite pose. In addition to a formal announcement, members of her family and representatives of national companies in which she was a major stockholder were included in the ceremony. As promised Marilee was kept informed of how her funds were being used, but organizers also arranged an individual meeting between Marilee and one of the senior officers to review the accounts and answer questions.

Her expectations were exceeded through deliberate work. She continued to be an important and vital donor. Her gifts amounted to more than $1 million, and she was grateful and proud to be a part of this institution.

The Lesson

When an agency exceeds donors' expectations, donors want to be part of their work. Determine appropriate donor expectations, then develop a strategy to exceed them. Build exceptional work into the plan. Know from the beginning what it will take to exceed the donor's expectations, and do not make promises that cannot be kept or surpassed.

Fund raisers tend to underestimate donors' expectations. Affluent older donors are particularly accustomed to excellent service. What may seem exceptional to someone from a younger generation may simply be normal to people of their parents' generation. Become familiar with a higher standard of service and exceed even your own expectations.

Dig the Well Before You Get Thirsty

The Principle

Harvey Mackay coined the popular admonition to "dig the well before you get thirsty." In philanthropy, this translates into building deep relationships before soliciting gifts. Often, solicitors become overly eager when they hear about someone with financial means. They solicit the gift too quickly and usually end up disappointed.

The Story

For a long time, Jacob and Maureen had been modest, annual donors to an environmental agency. Although the couple had given many financial gifts, neither had ever visited the agency, nor had they been contacted personally.

Eventually, the agency initiated a calling program. Jacob and Maureen were contacted by Sarah, the executive director, and informed of the importance of their gifts toward achieving this group's strong environmental goals. Jacob and Maureen really appreciated the communication. Even though the couple had only one conversation with Sarah, she left a positive impression and made them feel important and valued. For the next several years, Sarah was a frequent visitor in their home, providing them regular updates.

Later, the agency faced a serious crisis that created an urgent need for $300,000. Sarah called Jacob and Maureen and shared the situation with them, explaining the dilemma and outlining the financial needs. The couple was more than willing to contribute $200,000 toward the cause. In doing so, Jacob said, "Sarah, you have shared with us what was going on regarding your work there. For the last several years, you have been especially good at letting us know exactly how our gifts were helping to make a difference. Now that the agency has a crisis, we see it as our crisis, as well. We are ready to step forward and do what we can to be a part of the solution."

The Lesson

Mackay's popular book *Dig the Well Before You Get Thirsty* emphasizes the building and reinforcing of relationships as a major source of support in times of crisis. The time to build is when things are going well. Solid relationships are an agency's best wall of defense. Build high, build wide and build strong.

Nobody Wants to Give Money Away

The Principle

Nobody wants to give money away. Philanthropy works because millions of people want to change other people's lives. Even though Americans are heavily exposed to philanthropy, very few have been inspired to give significantly. The road to successful fund raising is littered with fund raisers who have solicited a donation without first determining if the donor is interested.

Another common mistake is to make presumptions about the loyalties of a donor without continued cultivation of the relationship. A donor who has given one large gift will not always direct future gifts to the same institution. Fund raisers who take donors for granted find themselves bereft of subsequent gifts. Appreciation and cultivation do not end with a donation and a receipt.

The Story

William donated more than $10 million to his favorite charity. His endowment gift was one of the largest ever received in the history of that nonprofit agency. William also mentioned the possibility of an even larger gift to the organization in the future. In time, the staff of the agency changed. William's personal association with the agency diminished.

The new leadership of the agency learned that William had previously considered giving a gift of up to $100 million. Unfortunately, the new leaders did not establish a relationship with William to help him understand the important differences such a large gift could make. Instead, the leaders focused on the agency's short-term needs.

A large portion of the desired $100 million would come from William's estate, but the agency's leaders did not want to wait for William's death. The leaders told him that what they really wanted was a gift that could immediately benefit the agency. This attitude is obviously deplorable, but it can easily slip into an agency's fund-raising mentality.

Afterward, it was easy for William to decide against making another gift to this nonprofit agency. Even ten years later, it was still firmly settled in William's mind that it was his money, and he was not going to be told what to do with it. He alone would choose *who* would get it and *when*.

The Lesson

Repeat giving occurs because earlier gifts have been valued, cultivated, and appreciated.

Recognize The Retired Elite

The Principle

One-third of retirees constitute the "retired elite." This description is given to retirees who have at least three sources of income: Social Security, a job-related pension, and some additional source. These retirees may not consider themselves the "elite," but through steady saving and wise investing, that is exactly what they have become.

The Story

Arden was a retired school administrator. In a meeting about his potential involvement in a fund-raising campaign, Arden offered, "I make more money now than I did when I was working." He had worked in the same school district for many years and had risen to the highest ranks of school administration. Along with Social Security, he had a good pension program. Arden also had personal savings and had purchased property. Careful money management allowed Arden to give $1 million to the school district's foundation. At his death, a gift of $3 million was designated for a variety of other charitable needs. Arden had not inherited any money, but he was certainly a member of the retired elite.

The Lesson

Retirees can be good prospects for gift solicitations. While many retirees feel limited by what they perceive as a fixed income, further investigation usually reveals a pension, property and other investments that can be creatively used for charitable giving.

You Don't Need an 800-Pound Gorilla

The Principle

One bit of advice typically given to an organization considering a fund-raising effort is, "Don't start without an 800-pound gorilla." Many think that without a heavyweight from the community's top leadership on board, the effort will go nowhere. In reality, however, this is not true. If it were as easy as finding a "big hitter," every fund-raising venture would succeed or fail on that basis alone. While community leadership is important, other factors play a greater role in achieving fund-raising objectives. Vital factors include:

1. **Committed Board Members.** A board member's commitment must exceed a general acknowledgment that the institution is worthwhile and deserving of support. Board members must participate in creating a case statement that correctly identifies the purpose of the effort. They should be among the first people solicited. They set the tone for the fund-raising effort.

2. **Steering Committee.** Members of the steering committee and constituency should have indicated intense support for the operation. As the effort unfolds, it is important to determine to what extent these individuals can support the agency.

3. **Development of the Case Statement.** The case statement must be developed as a cooperative effort by all those involved. This initial statement can be amended, improved and adjusted as the project develops, right up to the time of the public announcement. At that point, it becomes the fund-raising canon.

4. **Leadership Commitment.** The leadership should be sought first within the organization—from the board of directors, steering committee, advisory groups.

5. **Training.** A good training program discusses the fundamentals of fund raising, gives a clear picture of how gifts are made and delineates giving options.

6. **Prospect Identification.** Prospect identification combines the seemingly contradictory elements of casting a big net and then inspecting the catch selectively.

7. **Timeliness and Organization.** A timetable keeps things moving. Organization keeps things moving in the right direction.

8. **Donor Involvement.** Donors need to be actively involved in the effort and should be kept up-to-date on the progress.

9. **Recognition and Appreciation.** Recognition and appreciation should center on the donor's relationship to the organization. Make sure that personalizing your thanks means more than having it monogrammed.

10. **Follow-through.** People tend to remember how things finished more readily than how they began. Stay memorable.

11. **Victory.** Continually apprise the constituency of the fund-raising progress and anticipate the success ahead.

The Story

A Girl Scout council needed a service center, camp development and an endowment fund. Originally, they were advised to lower their expectations because they lacked the "800-pound gorilla." Yet two-and-a-half years later the council moved into its new facility. The council's successful campaign raised $2 million—nearly double what originally had been projected. Of the Girl Scouts' top ten gifts from individuals, seven were from women or foundations run by or for women.

Another example of maximizing philanthropy without a heavy hitter on the board comes from a local children's center. This agency had never discussed a major gifts effort, let alone a capital campaign, but succeeded in raising $1.3 million over a $1.2 million goal for a new building and endowment. The center was not a United Way agency, and its profile in the community was minimal. Yet, the center's leadership mobilized their prospects to raise this substantial sum. Out of 43 gifts to this campaign, less than a half-dozen came from businesses or foundations and represented less than 25 percent of the total. This campaign succeeded due to the empowerment of its leadership.

The Lesson

Successful fund-raising efforts occur when the above factors are present, the need is well established and can be documented, the organization has a good and valued reputation and the agency's leadership takes advantage of its strengths through full utilization of its opportunities. Even without the "gorilla."

The Integrated Campaign for Hesston College

The beauty of the Hesston College campus—its landscaping, carefully placed buildings and network of direct sidewalks—comes from decades of painstaking planning. Throughout the school's history, administrators have placed a high priority on campus design. The first campus plan was developed in the 1920s. Additional plans were drafted in 1964, 1976 and 1988.

The Campus Plan Update for the 90s challenged the Board of Overseers and administrators of Hesston College to seek funds totaling $20,300,000. That amount would provide for renovations and updates to existing buildings, underwrite additions to enable the College to use existing space more efficiently, and meet the requirements of the Americans with Disabilities Act (ADA). New construction plans called for a theater/recital hall/classroom building and the addition of a facility for the nursing program. Proposed renovations included the Mary Miller Library, the administration building, dormitories and athletic fields.

The College has a policy of securing an additional 50 percent of the cost of new construction as a building endowment. For example, the cost of Mary Miller Library—which calls for a 5,200-square-foot addition, entry reconstruction, lower level and main floor renovations, and upgrades to the heating and cooling system—was estimated at $2,225,000. Of this amount, $750,000 was the cost of new construction. Therefore, the building endowment was $375,000.

Hesston's leaders say that with the continual development of the campus, they intend to make Hesston College a better place for students to live and learn and a better place for faculty to teach.

Establishing an Integrated Campaign™

Hesston College was an ideal candidate for instituting an Integrated Campaign™. Their Partners program was raising about a million dollars annually. This represented about 13 percent of their operating budget. They could not afford to move these annual funds from operating to capital needs.

The College received estate gifts with minimal effort on their part. These gifts went into an endowment that could not be used for operational needs. The College was concerned that its needs were not being considered by many as a part of their estate plans.

An Integrated Campaign™ simply means considering the economic impact each significant donor can have on the financial vitality of the institution. **That is, what level of annual, program, capital and endowment support each donor should be asked to contribute.**

"The goal of $20,300,000 for us at Hesston College seemed very formidable," admits Loren Swartzendruber, Hesston's president, "We are a small college and had never attempted anything nearly that large."

Hesston College has a long history of Mennonite tradition and strong giving although its donor base is relatively small. After a careful study, its fund-raising consultants recommended that organizers break the financial goal into a three-phase campaign.

"There are three ways in which splitting the campaign has helped," Swartzendruber explains. "First, it enables us to return to donors for a second request. Second, it helps with timing because there are some donors who were unable to commit to Phase I due to other commitments. Third, it has enabled us to go to major foundations a second time in the campaign. Some major foundations will allow you to submit requests only every two years."

Enhancing Excellence Campaign: Phase 1

Phase I raised nearly $8 million by 1997. A gift of $750,000 from the Mabee Foundation and a $500,000 gift from an Indiana family were major catalysts for the success of Phase I.

"The campaign goal was based on the estimated cost of *The Campus Plan Update for the '90s*. Endowment needs were taken from the strategic plan developed by the College," Swartzendruber says. "In addition, Hartsook and Associates estimated a realistic goal for us to achieve. We are still on track to have a new campus by the year 2003. If we're able to achieve that, every building will either be new or will have been renovated in the past 20 years. That is a major challenge for us, but with the generosity of many friends and alumni, we believe that goal is attainable."

Frequently, donors were asked to continue their annual gifts at a higher level while considering capital and estate gifts. As a result of this strategy, as much as 20 percent of the annual fund is already committed for the next several years. Though they encountered no real obstacles, they learned about patience. According to Arliss Swartzendruber, campaign director, "As far as our lead gift prospects, the timing was not always quite right. We had to be patient. One lead donor came back a year later with a significant gift while another is making a substantial gift to Phase II."

Arliss also concedes that funds are limited and the competition is fierce. "Most donors receive many, many requests, which makes the impact of the case statement critical."

Volunteer Leadership

Hesston College relies on a small, but dedicated Board of Overseers. "Our Board has only 12 members," says President Swartzendruber. "They are not selected specifically for their ability to give financially. That has limited the financial support of the Board, but Board members have been very encouraging. They have provided a great deal of affirmation for the campaign and its accomplishments. Some have conferred planned, outright or deferred gifts. We had one gift of $1 million from a Board member who wished to remain anonymous."

Campaign Director Swartzendruber is quick to compliment his volunteers and staff. "I have a campaign coordinator who is tremendous about following up on details. She deals with issues and tasks related to the steering committee as well as the development and renovation of facilities. This allows us to work with donors and prospective donors."

Hesston College has been guided by a volunteer steering committee of 45 people from across the U.S. and Ontario, Canada. Phase I campaign co-chairs, Howard Hershberger of Kansas and Wilbur Bontrager of Indiana, were helpful in chairing committee meetings held on campus. They coordinated and led regional meetings in their areas as well. In the Phase II portion of the campaign, Bontrager is serving as honorary chair, along with several other persons. Hershberger continues as co-chair and he is joined by Jan Roth of Hesston as co-chair.

Fund-raising stewardship at Hesston College is conservative. A strict policy says that no construction project will begin until funds are committed. Donor recognition is in a modest, appreciative manner.

"As far as recognition is concerned, we have named buildings for donors or to acknowledge persons who have made significant contributions through their lives to Hesston College," says President Swartzendruber. "Other acknowledgments for gifts have included naming conference rooms, putting up plaques, and giving pieces of art created by a retired professor."

The Next Phase

As Hesston College moves into Phase II, President Swartzendruber feels more confident in his expectations of the fund-raising process.

"We expect the gifts to come from an expanded donor base. We have 40 lead gift prospects for Phase II, and only 13 of those contributed to Phase I. We continue to find ways to use volunteers meaningfully," said President Swartzendruber.

Integrity: Do What You Say You'll Do

It's the Donor's Money

The Principle

By law, when a gift transfers to an institution, the donor relinquishes control over its use. However, a donor rarely is asked only once for a gift. Managing the gift efficiently and appropriately is critical to maintaining the donor's trust. As the donor's sense of ownership in the organization grows her desire to make additional gifts to the agency increases.

While an agency might prefer to receive unrestricted gifts—packages without strings—a gift given to a general cause will normally be smaller than one for something specific. Prospective donors appreciate knowing about the project. They like to know how the money will be used and what it is expected to produce. The result of providing such information typically is a much larger gift.

The Story

Marilyn was a fast-food philanthropist who owned and operated several Dairy Queen restaurants. Her business meant more to her than simply a way of making money. What Marilyn really enjoyed was the active practice of business. She valued the young people she hired, always caring how they were treated and showing genuine concern for their well-being.

Later in life, Marilyn was approached about making a gift to an agency for children. She had numerous questions about how her gift would be used. She knew that her money could make a difference in the lives of children, but she wanted the specifics of where each and every dollar would be allotted. Without hesitation, the agency did everything possible to answer her questions. They broke down their annual operating budget and identified specific uses for her donation. As a result, she felt supremely confident that her gift of $400,000 would be used according to her wishes—providing training, materials, and transportation. Marilyn became the first woman to become a member of the board of this agency. Later, she chaired it.

The Lesson

A donor who grasps the actual use of a gift is usually inspired to give more. Even after the money has been deposited and the tax receipt issued, a fund raiser is wise to remember that it was the donor's money before it was solicited, it was the donor's money when it was given, and in an important sense, it still is the donor's money.

Be Truthful

The Principle

Being truthful extends light-years beyond the realm of merely not lying. It means rejecting exaggeration and misleading statements. It means presenting proposals and strategies that can actually be executed for the projected costs.

Donors whose hard work and ingenuity have allowed them to acquire enough wealth to give away millions of dollars know the value of a quality project. No one at this tier of affluence is looking for a bargain. They can quickly surmise the difference between what can and cannot be produced with a certain amount of capital.

Fund raisers who have a reputation of suggesting a low-dollar gift and a high-dollar project are quickly seen for what they are—inaccurate. Nothing is worse than encouraging a donor to dream a big dream, promising to bring that dream to fruition, and then, after the donor has upheld his end of the bargain, delivering an inferior product. Those who operate in this way find that their donor relations quickly wear thin.

The Story

Morris, an athletic director, visited a major sports enthusiast to request a gift of $100,000 to assist in the building of skyboxes at a football stadium. The donor, Caroline, questioned Morris about the details of how the donation would be used. Morris painted an elaborate picture of all that this $100,000 gift would accomplish.

As Morris lost himself describing the grandeur of the box-to-be, Caroline asked Morris just how many gifts were being solicited to achieve these lofty goals. "Only five," the fund raiser replied. Quickly calculating what could actually be done with $500,000, Caroline questioned how such majestic feats could be accomplished with such a modest investment. Unwavering, Morris assured Caroline that it could be done. After carefully considering the proposal, Caroline declined.

Six weeks later, Morris returned to Caroline's office, tail between his legs. Morris had already secured $300,000 of the $500,000 he had planned to raise. After meeting with architects and contractors, Morris realized that the project could not be accomplished for under $1 million. Now, he wanted to talk to Caroline about a $500,000 gift. This larger gift, more in line with the actual need, would give Caroline the leadership position in this project and the opportunity to choose its name.

Under this more realistic plan, Caroline was willing to come on board, but she wanted Morris to know that in the future, the economic research should be done thoroughly before a gift is solicited. The $500,000 gift was secured, and Morris learned a fundamental lesson.

The Lesson

Truthfulness earns credibility. Dishonesty leaves nothing to build on in the future. Donors at this level are not looking for a bargain. Honesty, careful research and a thorough knowledge of the project are essential to securing major gifts.

Most Wealth Is Earned, Not Inherited

The Principle

More than 80 percent of millionaires have earned, rather than inherited, their wealth. These first generation millionaires typically view their wealth differently than those who have inherited wealth. Those who began with little and have used their earnings to save substantial amounts usually have no sense of obligation concerning philanthropy. This is also true of people who generate their own wealth in addition to receiving an inheritance.

The remaining 20 percent of millionaires have a different outlook. Those whose wealth is passed to them from previous generations often inherit a sense of *noblesse oblige*, which includes an obligation toward philanthropy.

Fund raisers should be aware of these different outlooks and vary their solicitations accordingly. For example, millionaires of first-generation wealth are more likely to:

1. Ensure that their families have enough resources for the future;
2. Express wealth in a socially favorable manner;
3. Have a limited understanding of the difference between what a $10 million gift and a $100 million gift could accomplish;
4. Decline solicitations so frequently that they appear immune to requests;

5. Gain an interest in philanthropy if encouraged to view philanthropy as giving back to benefit others.

The Story

As the leadership of a hospital considered their prospects for a major effort, they took the easy first step of looking at those families that had given to them for years. The hospital was confident of the wealth of these prospects because they knew each member of the family had inherited wealth. What they came to learn, though, was that in many cases, the wealth of these families had not grown appreciably and was not as great as they had assumed.

However, when they reviewed the list of individuals who recently had benefitted from the hospital, they were pleasantly surprised to discover the founder of a "hot" software production company, the owner of a national chain of assisted living facilities, the family that took the hometown bar and grill and made it a national name, and many other entrepreneurs. They understood that those people viewed their wealth differently from those who had inherited wealth and needed to be approached differently.

Understanding the values of the first generation wealthy was important to the hospital's success.

The Lesson

Respect the differences between people who earn their wealth and those for whom inherited wealth is a way of life. Invest the time to develop the donor's understanding of philanthropy, always listening to the donor carefully. Do not assume that what has worked in past efforts will work again.

The Hand
That Rocks
The Checkbook

The Principle

Eighty-seven percent of all wealth ultimately goes through the hands of women, an often-overlooked fact that is finally being recognized in fund-raising circles. Traditionally, fund raising has been geared toward men. An institution that understands that women control and distribute wealth enhances opportunities for philanthropy.

The Story

Jeanette was a wealthy woman who kept a low profile. She cared a great deal about an institution for adults with physical disabilities because her only child had received many years of support from this agency. After her son's death, she moved away and lost personal contact with the institution.

During a major fund drive, the agency's fund raisers contacted Jeanette since she had regularly given modest gifts over a long period of time. What the agency did not know was that Jeanette had maintained a modest lifestyle while holding a large family inheritance. By this time, Jeanette had outlived everyone else in her family. Her control of this wealth was not well known and certainly not appreciated.

During the initial reacquaintance meeting, Jeanette shared that she was prepared to give a gift in excess of $10 million. Further, she was not interested in tax advantages because she felt that taxes were appropriate and necessary. Jeanette was convinced that her gift would be used effectively and was grateful to the institution for this opportunity to support their efforts. The agency's fund raisers were stunned speechless.

The Lesson

Solicitation strategies have commonly centered on men. It is time to rethink those strategies. What are some of the reasons women give? How can women best be recognized and appreciated for their generosity?

Fund raisers should be aware that:

1. Forty-three percent of all individuals in the U.S. with assets of more than $1 million are women.
2. Women make up 35 percent of the country's shareholders.
3. Sixty percent of the wealth in this country is owned and managed by women.
4. Women-owned businesses employ millions of people in the United States, one-third more than those employed by Fortune 500 firms.
5. Of 3.3 million Americans classified as "wealth holders" by the Internal Revenue Service, 41.2 percent were women.
6. Sixty percent of persons 65 years of age and older are women.
7. Women outnumber men nearly three to one after the age of 85.
8. Eighty-seven percent of all wealth passes through the hands of a woman.

In light of these realities, it is essential to recognize the critical role of women in the philanthropic process.

How Did You Become Successful?

The Principle

The cultivation process can be extremely educational for the fund raiser who approaches it with eagerness and interest. Open-ended questions are a great way to gain insight into the donor's interests, concerns and values. "How did you become successful?" is a powerful question to introduce early in the relationship. This strategy of asking, listening, learning and responding appropriately is the key to successful solicitation.

The Story

University fund raisers solicited Emelio, a successful businessman, for a gift to his alma mater. Because Emelio was an entrepreneur with an uncanny grasp of finance, marketing and management, the fund raisers initially assumed that his gift would go toward the university's business school. Realizing that situations are seldom what they seem, one astute fund raiser, Keith, asked Emelio how he had become successful. Keith was not merely repeating a formula; he was genuinely interested.

Emelio responded gladly to Keith's question, "What this school taught me was how to write a good letter. I learned how to stand up before a group and make a presentation. I learned how to sell." Emelio had attended college in the late 1930s and early 1940s. Since that time, the communications program had suffered setbacks.

Keith later came back to Emelio with a solicitation proposal in support of the business school as expected, but also with an innovative plan to revitalize the university's school of communications. Emelio was excited by both the concept and the request, making a multi-million-dollar commitment to the school of communications which now bears his name. If Keith had followed the fund-raising advice of others, or if he had talked and not listened, the university might have received a more modest sum. Because Keith asked and discovered what was important to Emelio, a major gift was secured.

The Lesson

Ask people how they became successful. Listen intently. If it matters to them, it should matter to the fund raiser.

Saving The Best For Last

The Principle

Everyone understands the power of a first impression. However, it is equally meaningful to leave a lasting impression.

The Story

Margaret is the field representative for a national fund-raising effort on behalf of disabled children. As part of this work, Margaret travels on the road or in the air virtually every day. The demands of constant travel are very taxing, but Margaret understands that she represents the energy of the agency. Because of the distance between prospective donors and the agency, donors must pick up the enthusiasm and importance of their giving through Margaret. She understands the relevance of her first impression in securing donor support and financial gifts. No matter what her travel schedule, she continues to convey a level of excitement that adequately illustrates the agency's vital work.

One Friday, after a long week of meetings, Margaret flew to visit with a donor, Noreen, whom she had met several times and knew fairly well. Margaret told Noreen about all that was going on at the agency, including some things that had happened in the lives of the children. Margaret related the agency's appreciation and gratefulness for Noreen's continued generosity. As Margaret prepared to leave, Noreen inquired, "Will you tell me another story?" Margaret was surprised because she had already shared several events. Noreen continued, "I need to have a story to hang on to as you go. I need to hear something with a happy ending, so that I feel like I am really helping someone. This is what keeps me going."

Tired as she was, Margaret realized how important it was to end their time together on a positive note. With fresh enthusiasm, Margaret related a story of a child who, with the help of the agency, had overcome incredible obstacles. Noreen was touched by what she heard, and her tears were for joy and thankfulness that she could be a part of this effort. Margaret and Noreen parted with mutual admiration and esteem. Noreen had heard what she had needed to hear, and Margaret had learned an invaluable lesson.

The Lesson

Do not just leave. Leave a memory. Make a lasting impression by saving the best for last and making the visit memorable.

Never Stop the Presses

The Principle

Continued communication with donors, benefactors and friends is critical to maintaining a good relationship. A newsletter is one component. Special bulletins, telephone calls, e-mail, websites and regular contact are all important aspects of keeping a connection with those who care about the organization.

The Story

Several years ago the leaders of a youth recreation agency decided to quit sending their newsletter to former members and volunteers to save money. They reasoned that those dollars would be better spent on youth programs.

As a result, Mike, a former member who had volunteered when his sons were involved, did not hear from his local agency for many years. The agency continued to send its newsletter to current volunteers and former board members, but Mike fell outside those parameters. Mike cared about the agency, but because he was no longer receiving any information from or about the agency, he felt that they no longer cared whether he knew what was going on.

After years of use, the local youth camp facilities and service center were in disrepair. Their annual fund covered the essential services and program costs, but little funding was available for maintenance and virtually nothing for improvements. A young boy who was using the poorly maintained facilities was injured. Although his injuries were minor, the parents took legal action against the agency.

When the details of this lawsuit became public, Mike became aware of the challenges facing the agency. In conversations with his son Steve, a successful entrepreneur in a distant city, Mike shared his deep concerns. Unknown to Mike, Steve called the executive director. He told him that once the lawsuit was settled, he would make a gift to support renovating the camp facilities. He chose to wait so that none of these funds would be put at risk by the legal action. The agency's insurance company was already negotiating a settlement that soon reached resolution. Steve then made a gift of more than $1.5 million for the renovation of the camp.

Through regular communication with Mike, the renovation might have occurred earlier, and the injury might not have happened at all. Mike appreciated his son's gift, but he made it clear to the agency's leadership, "You need to keep in touch with folks like me, so that we know how to help."

The Lesson

While we cannot communicate with everyone, we must be strategic and thoughtful in finding out who is interested and why. Keeping the agency's information in front of these people is very important. Never stop the presses.

Celebrate Success

The Principle

Celebrating success is not the same as bragging about gifts. Success does not belong to one person but is shared by the donors and the agency. The joy comes from being a vital part of an important agency, not just from securing gifts.

Public announcements about fund-raising campaigns are not the trumpet calls that stir the desire of multitudes to give millions of dollars. However, these announcements can notify an agency's constituency that the project is making important progress or nearing completion.

The Story

A major specialty hospital in a large city was conducting a multi-million-dollar endowment and programmatic campaign with a modest capital component. The hospital fund-raising staff had worked for several years to prepare for the campaign and had been in the implementation stage of the campaign plan for nearly three years. They were approaching the $40 million mark.

At their annual banquet, they publicly kicked off the campaign and announced that $10 million had yet to be raised. Also, they announced an exciting opportunity to receive matching funds for endowed medical teaching chairs. Each endowed chair represented $1.1 million, which the state would match to create a $2.2 million chair. The organizers followed the announcement of the campaign with the identification of those chairs that had already been endowed. Darrin, the trustee of a major foundation in the community, came to Phillip, the hospital's executive director. Darrin was intrigued by the idea of endowing a chair and was very interested in how this might happen.

Phillip emphasized to Darrin that the chair had to be funded in its entirety before the state would match the funds. Additionally, Phillip let Darrin know that there were a variety of ways this could be done. Caught up in the excitement of the growing success of this project and the added value of the state's matching funds, Darrin's foundation offered the $1.1 million necessary to endow the chair.

The chair was established, and as a result, the campaign gained momentum.

The Lesson

Throughout major fund-raising activities, keep the agency's constituents aware of successes and exciting possibilities. A distinct, yet subtle, difference must be recognized between the enthusiastic sharing of success and premature (and possibly inflated) statements regarding the status of the campaign.

This delicate balance can be achieved by judging the situation with honesty and humility. Celebrating true milestones can encourage others who hear about the campaign to jump on board with gifts.

Giving begets giving.

Seven Feelings Every Donor Should Have

The Principle

The donor has seven needs to which the fund raiser needs to be responsive.

The Donor's Need to Be...	**The Fund Raiser needs to...**
Heard	Listen
Understood	Empathize
Liked	Validate
Respected	Honor
Helped	Serve
Appreciated	Commend
Valued	Esteem

All seven are important criteria for measuring the strength of association between an institution and its donors. To the degree that these needs are met, the alliance will be strong and lasting. If they are neglected, the connection will be weak.

For the most part, these are simple relational skills. In philanthropy they are crucial. Donors involve themselves financially and emotionally with an institution that they can only influence and will never own. This is a huge offering and fund raisers should respond in kind. Rather than trying to appear to listen, understand, like, respect, help, appreciate, and value a donor, a fund raiser is wiser to genuinely do these things. The donor deserves no less.

The Story

Seldom does a donor experience all seven of these feelings in one meeting, but it happened with Aaron. Aaron had been a major donor to a local children's museum. Over the years, he and his wife had given several nice gifts to the museum. Charlotte, the museum's director of development, had an appointment to visit with Aaron about a major gift that she was fairly confident that Aaron and his wife would give. After preparing for her presentation, just three hours before the early morning appointment, Charlotte learned that Aaron's wife had died. The death was not unexpected, but was nonetheless difficult. Charlotte called Aaron's office to extend sympathy and to cancel the appointment. Much to Charlotte's surprise, Aaron wanted to keep the appointment.

During their meeting, Aaron expressed how important the children's museum had been to his wife and him. He recounted a couple of stories of how they had appreciated the marvelous work of the museum and seen its resulting impact on children. Charlotte reminded Aaron of how important their gifts had been at a critical point two years ago. She commented that everyone in the community knew of the couple's support of the museum.

After several reflective moments, Charlotte said, "You know, I was prepared today to talk about a $3 million gift to launch our new programming initiative, but now is probably not the best time for you to be considering such decisions. You have more important things on your mind right now."

Without hesitation, Aaron responded, "No, in fact I want to hear about your plans. Today is the best day for us to talk."

Charlotte proceeded to discuss and ultimately solicit the gift. Aaron immediately committed the $3 million. Aaron expressed his appreciation for Charlotte's willingness to listen and to help him focus on something that would continue his wife's legacy.

The Lesson

Donor satisfaction is more measurable than might be expected. Use these seven criteria to gage the strength of the relationship between the donor and the institution. On a scale of one to five (a weak relationship to a strong one), assess the status of the top 50 donors. Strategically build relationships to last. When these actions do not come naturally, the fund raiser needs to adjust his attitude or change his profession.

Peanut Butter And Jelly Sandwiches

The Principle

When fund raisers schedule a meeting with a prospective donor, they often feel that they need to arrange the finest accommodations and feature the most expensive presentations. In many cases, this is the right approach. Sometimes, however, the situation calls for something different.

The Story

Shelby was the director of development for a children's museum in the southwestern United States. In her effort to cultivate donors and actively involve them in the agency, she conducted a weekly luncheon at the museum. On the menu were peanut butter and jelly sandwiches, served with juice and a cookie. There were other options for those who preferred a different lunch, but the peanut butter and jelly sandwiches highlighted the reason for the museum's work—the children. The donors loved it. Shelby's memorable and meaningful first contact with prospective donors led to a number of large gifts.

The Lesson

Sincerity is always more impressive than pomp and circumstance. Nothing is wrong in doing things with excellence. Quality expresses respect, which can only enhance an agency's reputation. However, things done primarily for show will appear pretentious and artificial. Do not waste time or money building a facade. Show the donors what is real.

When tempted to spend money on Waterford crystal and Lenox china, or to entertain at the fanciest restaurants and most notable country clubs, remember the children's museum and their peanut butter and jelly sandwiches.

Remember The Five Thank Yous

The Principle

Saying thank you is not only proper, it can be profitable. When people feel appreciated, they are more likely to keep giving. In the afterglow of a successful gift or campaign, the importance of thanking others can be overlooked. A fund raiser needs to convey thanks in an authentic and timely way.

1. A thank you to the donor,
2. A thank you to the staff supporting the effort,
3. A thank you to employers,
4. A thank you to those assisting in identification and cultivation,
5. A personal thank you to oneself for hard work and thoroughness.

The Story

Sharon, a college president, once offered a memorable thank you. Sharon's college had a long-standing association with a well-known philanthropic family, but because of a rift with the patriarch, who also was an alumnus, the relationship had been strained for the last 20 years. Sharon had been allowed to meet with the family leader, and things went well. They discovered many common interests and began building a good relationship. The man made a small gift to the university and later, after visiting the campus, gave the university $1.5 million.

When Sharon learned of this large gift, the first people she called into her office were the maintenance employees. She appreciated the work they had done to prepare for their guest's visit, and she wanted them to personally know of the result. She expressed her thanks for their efforts in making the campus such a beautiful place. Their conscientious care had prepared the way for the college in receiving this magnificent gift.

The Lesson

Give thanks sincerely and liberally. Besides thanking the donor, do not forget to thank all those who played a part in making the gift a reality: secretaries, employers, program staff members, vendors and suppliers, volunteers, and others. Finally, a pat on the back is in order.

Offer Your Donor Control

The Principle

Most millionaires are accustomed to being in charge of their money. After years of careful management of businesses and investments, they are accustomed to being fully involved and informed. It would be altogether unnatural to expect these donors to turn over their hard-earned money without retaining a voice in the giving schedule or other aspects of the gift.

Many even try to provide for some level of management posthumously. A recent study of final tax returns revealed that many men (if not most) who leave money in an estate plan do so through a family foundation. This hands-on habit dies hard.

The Story

John owned a trucking company in a small community. Community leaders asked him to donate $1 million for a community center. At first John did not feel he could make that level of gift. Hoping to overcome John's objections, the community center's planners offered a personalized strategy endorsed by area leaders. This arrangement was much more in line with John's personality and the ways of dealing with money common among entrepreneurial businessmen.

The plan called for John to give $1 million over a period of five years. However, John was free to set the timing of payments and the tempo of his giving instead of making equal and regular installments. In a year that business was going well, he could give liberally. In a year when business was slow, he would not have to give anything. Because he was offered this level of control, John agreed to donate the $1 million.

The Lesson

Find ways to offer donors control over their giving. Besides offering donors control over timing of gifts, another possibility would be to allow the donor to select a supervisory committee that oversees the distribution of a gift.

The Donor Is Always... The Donor

The Principle

When it comes to working with donors, a successful fund raiser should clearly understand the two most important rules:

1. The donor is always right!
2. If in doubt, refer to rule #1.

Of course, this tongue-in-cheek axiom does not mean that the donor never makes a mistake. It means that despite mistakes or short-comings, the donor is still the donor, and therefore deserves to be treated with the utmost graciousness and respect.

The Story

Ten million dollars fell off the table when a large university forgot whose money they were handling. Rachel and Keith were devoted alumni of this university. They were active in the basketball program and were always front and center cheering the team to victory. When presented with the idea of a new basketball arena, they jumped at the chance to provide the lead gift of $10 million. They were enthusiastic, but not foolish. Their demands were simple: build it, honor Keith's father, and complete it by the date specified.

Internal politics regarding design and location exist at most large universities, and the campus leadership's focus was distracted by this. Many egos were included and unfortunately became the heart of the project. The university needed to raise another $30 million to complete the private fund-raising component of the effort. Instead, the staff spent too much time celebrating the $10 million and not enough time seeking the other $30 million. Because the staff felt confident that the family was not obsessed by the completion date, they let time slip by. No other gifts were received, possibly none were solicited. The university's plan was to go to the legislature for the balance if the private funding was not in place. University leaders did not talk to the donors for weeks, months. At one point an entire year went by without contacting donors regarding their progress.

Since the community knew of the $10 million gift, the university believed Keith and Rachel would never consider retracting it. They were wrong. When it became apparent beyond a doubt that the university was not going to make the date, they pulled their gift.

The Lesson

When something goes wrong, as it invariably will, someone must take responsibility and humbly and quickly put things back on track. It will be much less frustrating if a fund raiser sees this as part of his job description. Making the necessary effort to keep a donor content is not the icing on the cake—it is the cake. The task of a skilled fund raiser is to keep the donor satisfied.

Don't Count on Special Events

The Principle

The public generally believes that great sums of money are raised annually through various galas, golf tournaments, auctions and other events. Rarely is this true. Rather than serving as a fast track to reaching a financial goal, special events can become quicksand to a fund-raising effort.

Special events take an immense amount of preparation time. Although such events can raise moderate amounts, the financial return is rarely enough to justify the investment of time and energy. For every event that is an exception to this rule, ten others fail to raise enough money to cover expenses. These events chew up a substantial amount of professional and volunteer time. They may also cause discouragement, draining momentum from the campaign.

For this reason, it is important to think of special events primarily as a way to cultivate donor and prospect relationships. As a relationship-building tool, the special event can be powerful.

The Story

Not long ago, a museum hosted a cricket event. It was an idea of grand proportions. The evening prior to the cricket match, there would be an elegant gala featuring silent and open auctions. The next day there was to be a cricket match on beautiful new grounds. The agency expected to reap hundreds of thousands of dollars, based on the financial backgrounds of those interested in both cricket and the organization.

Months before the event, the fund raisers organized committees, gathered volunteers, solicited groups, and secured underwriting for the event. As the day of the event approached, invitations were sent and the grounds were groomed. At this point, the event had already consumed enormous quantities of time on the part of the director of development and her staff.

Hundreds participated in the match, gala and auction. The combined events, which grossed several hundred thousand dollars, netted only $40,000 for the organization.

Christine, the chair of the board, complimented the whole event. Privately she confided that the supporters of the event turned out to be either her friends or business associates. Of the several large auction items, Christine personally had purchased four. One item was a European vacation, which she had solicited as a gift to the gala's fund-raising event from a friend who owned a travel agency. Christine felt she would be obligated to reciprocate in the future when this friend, or one of her other friends, asked for similar support from her.

On paper, the event had raised $40,000 for the organization. In reality, Christine believed it actually cost her $200,000 in gifts and donations to other institutions. In retrospect, Christine would have preferred to give the organization the money outright and spared everyone hours of effort.

The Lesson

Any agency can benefit from periodic special events. In fact, it is probably a good idea for an institution to have an annual marquee event to broaden the support base for the agency. By making it annual much of the initial planning and work does not need to be repeated, and experience usually leads to efficiency. However, expectations for this event should focus on relationships built and cultivated, not on dollars raised.

Collaboration Times Three

Integrated Fund Raising Works for an Organization in its Infancy

Social service agencies increase in number every day making duplication of services a major source of concern for both non-profits and those who support them. Three Kansas City agencies, however, found a way to take the best each had to offer, combine their efforts and more fully address the needs of their constituents.

Administrators for the Children's Center for the Visually Impaired (CCVI)—an organization that provides specialized education for blind and visually impaired youngsters from birth to age seven, and Children's Therapeutic Learning Center (TLC)—an association which offers individualized education and therapy plans for children from birth to age six, agreed that there were often overlaps in the services they provided. With competition increasing among nonprofits, these two agencies agreed that they did not want to aggravate the problem but preferred to join forces to solve it. While each entity wanted to remain autonomous, sharing space and services seemed highly practical.

CCVI and Children's TLC wanted to meet another need as well. Many of the children they served had siblings with no disabilities. For parents of these children, that meant dropping off and picking up kids at two different locations, sometimes clear across town. They also wanted to provide opportunities for their students to interact with other children with disabilities, as well as children without disabilities. After defining their wants and needs, CCVI and Children's TLC began looking for a third partner to provide quality child-care services.

The YWCA of Kansas City, which became the first center-based child-care provider in 1975, was their partner of choice. All three agencies would share a facility while retaining separate administrative and financial functions. Through the collaboration, the Children's Center Campus (CCC) was born.

Though the partnership of the agencies would solve many problems, it would create a few as well. Of the three organizations, none had enough space to provide a permanent home for CCC. A new campus would have to be constructed. Plans called for a 50,000 square-foot building. Shared space would include a therapeutic pool, gymnasiums, cafeteria and kitchen, reception and waiting areas, and meeting, conference and staff rooms. Each agency would design its own classrooms, therapy rooms and offices.

A new building meant that a substantial amount of money would have to be raised. While administrators were prepared to launch a capital campaign, they soon learned that there were some concerns about creating yet another organization that would require community support.

"Several major donors insisted that they would not be supportive if creating CCC meant that they would have to feed another non-profit," says CCC fund-raising counsel, Bob Hartsook. Counsel recommended an Integrated Fund-Raising Campaign™ which would cover the costs of construction, endowments and annual funding. This would get the organization off to a solid start.

Utilizing three board members from each agency, CCC established its own board of directors to oversee the fund raising, building and management of the combined facility. After completing a thorough assessment of the plans, the consulting firm recommended a goal of $11 million.

"We started with another consulting firm,"explains Shirley Patterson, executive director of Children's TLC,"The first study recommended a goal of $5 million. When we got the new figure, we were concerned. But it quickly became evident that while it was more than double the initial assessment, this second goal was much more realistic."

One aspect of the campaign which complicated the entire process was the fact that the three agencies were not equally vested. CCVI and Children's TLC had each pledged a portion of their endowments toward meeting the $11 million goal. That left them with a more vested interest than the YWCA.

"For the YWCA, this is just one little part of their overall program," Dolembo says. "Their administrative offices would not be moving to the new facility. CCVI and Children's TLC, however, were both moving their administrative offices."

They looked to counsel for advice. "Hartsook helped us to establish a strategic alliance agreement to protect our endowment money," Dolembo says. "If we did not need to use it, we would get it back. We developed guidelines, prepared lease agreements, and essentially covered all the bases legally."

Though Dolembo says it was not a conscious decision, CCC never went public with their campaign. The $11 million dollars they received came from a small base of just 190 donors. That was a real plus.

"This non-public campaign meant that each agency could continue to solicit their own donors for the ongoing operational support necessary each year," Hartsook says. "Without that support, the agencies have a great building but no operating funds."

The success of the campaign, say organizers, stemmed from the hard work of the volunteers and the loyalty of patrons who had been served by one of the three agencies in the past. Certain large gifts were key.

"Several major gifts came from families who have been impacted by one of the agencies' work and others came from long-time board members," Hartsook notes. "Cultivation was critical."

Hallmark Cards was the first to contribute. Their gift of $865,000 would purchase the new site. The Hall Family Foundation gave an additional gift of $2.5 million which included $365,000 to acquire the property adjacent to the site.

The Halls were behind the campaign in other ways as well. Don and Adele Hall served as honorary co-chairs of the campaign, and David Hall had already been a member of the Board of CCVI for the past seven years.

"The endorsement of the Hall family is rather like the Good Housekeeping Seal of Approval in Kansas City," noted William Dunn, Sr., who co-chaired the capital campaign with Barbara Nelson.

Another prominent Kansas City family whose lives were touched came to the aid of CCC as well. Crosby Kemper, whose granddaughter, Cynthia Kemper Dietrich is a graduate of the Children's TLC program, donated $1 million.

Upon announcing their intent to purchase Boatmen's Banks, NationsBank was eager to make a strong statement regarding their commitment to the community. On the same day the new NationsBank signs were erected, Bill Nelson, president of NationsBank, Kansas City Region, announced a gift of $1 million to CCC.

Trustees of the Carolyn Doughty Fund decided to make CCC the recipient of their final gift. The $465,000 went to establish the Carolyn Doughty Recreational Center featuring a heated pool and playground. Volunteers played an important role in this cooperative effort, and their leadership and initiative were crucial to the success.

"We had a high caliber of volunteers," Dolembo says. "Our campaign co-chairs, Barbara Nelson and Bill Dunn, Sr., almost single-handedly raised the funds because they were so tied to the community. The co-chairs worked with the steering committee who were also an integral part of the process. In fact, one member of the steering committee, Mrs. Louis Ward, wrote a check for $1 million."

While CCC saw funds roll in without going public, they did run into a small hurdle near the end of the campaign.

"We were naive going into this goal," Dolembo admits. "There were things we did not allow for in the budget. Some of the items we forgot to include were furnishings, a security system, telephone systems and moving expenses.

"Our consultant had us identify what we should have included and estimated the cost," she continues. "We found that we needed in excess of $650,000 in addition to what still remained on our campaign goal. Combined, those figures left us with a little more than $1 million to raise. But there were also some places where we had saved money. Once all the numbers were reworked, we were left with only $835,000 yet to raise."

The final dollars came in, and Children's Center Campus became a reality on January 4, 1999. More than 300 children will call CCC their second home. Patterson credits their success to the fact that all three agencies were already established in the community.

"I've received calls from people saying, 'Why haven't you asked me for money?'" Patterson says. "Our history really helped us. The community knew us. We have all done good work over the years, and people know that we are credible. The fact that we were continually presenting ourselves as a threesome was positive. People saw that we were united."

Though the goal was easily reached in less than a year, organizers concede that the collaboration itself was not easy. Having an outside consultant who was so familiar with the fund-raising process—and who was able to offer an unbiased perspective throughout—was crucial to keeping everyone on track.

"There were some differences of opinion," Patterson admits. "They were primarily operational and philosophical—obviously not of the magnitude to stop the project."

"We knew the last dollars would be the hardest," Dolembo says. "But our confidence grew as the large gifts came in. It has been very exciting. Our consultant really kept our enthusiasm up and guided us when we were unsure."

Dolembo says the consultant often played devil's advocate as well. "He brought us down to reality. We all thought we had a really good chance at the Kresge Foundation grant, but he cautioned us not to get our hopes up. He had a lot of knowledge and expertise about the foundation community and knew the requirements of the various foundations. He directed us to the Mabee Foundation which resulted in a $1,250,000 capital grant."

In turn, the consultant gives kudos to the boards of the three agencies for their part, and adds that the 100 percent participation from each of the three boards sent a positive message to prospects."We offered to give the YWCA the option to pass on board support, but they stepped up to the table," Hartsook says. "This was really a team effort."

What We Learned:

The Children's Center Campaign offered some unique challenges and pointed out some important lessons.

1. Consider and address concerns head on. Prospective donors were concerned that establishing CCC would create another organization which would require their support, when, in essence, the cooperation of the three agencies actually eliminated duplication and reduced overhead.

2. Provide for the future. The Integrated™ approach not only provided capital funds, but also offered the organization a secure future through endowments and annual funding.

3. Use your organization's history as an asset. Call on those who know and respect your work in the community.

4. Enlist the best. Top-notch volunteers who really tackle the task of fund raising and have strong ties to the community may prove to be your biggest asset.

Putting the Gift Together

The Million-Dollar Mail Solicitation

The Principle

Direct mail is clearly not the way to solicit million-dollar gifts, but that is just what happened at one university. An agency should be sure the proper process of cultivation and solicitation is clearly explained to anyone involved in fund raising. Do not assume that everyone understands the basics.

The Story

President Bob thought of himself as a novice fund raiser. He allowed his various development officers to perform these duties for him, and they did well. At the same time, he was always available to support their efforts. But as he approached retirement, he felt it was time to close an important gift on his own. The development office suggested Adam as a good prospect for President Bob to cultivate and solicit for a major gift. Adam made a regular annual gift of $50,000 and had the potential to give a million dollars or more. Franklin, the vice president for development, already had a great relationship with Adam so Franklin met with Adam to discuss the upcoming solicitation and how it would be handled. He wanted Bob to have a successful solicitation experience.

During his meeting with Franklin, Adam agreed to give $50,000 annually for the next five years, plus a $1 million capital gift and a $1 million deferred gift for an endowment.

Later, Franklin met with Bob to give him some direction on closing the gift with Adam. He mentioned to Bob that he often used a letter to solidify a commitment and close the solicitation. It was a simple letter that outlined the provisions of the arrangement. The President, who had great confidence in his ability to communicate by letter, drafted the solicitation.

Not long after, Franklin got a call from Adam. Having been solicited on many occasions, Adam questioned Franklin about the letter he had just received in the mail. "Did you intend to solicit me for $2.25 million through the mail?"

Franklin quickly apologized to Adam for not clearly communicating the mechanics of the process to Bob. Franklin had intended for the letter to be taken and delivered by hand when Bob and Adam met. Adam made the gift despite the miscommunication, but the president learned an important lesson.

The Lesson

Make sure all aspects of the fund-raising process are clearly delineated and communicated. Do not let new fund raisers learn expensive lessons through trial and error.

Look for Diamonds In the Rough

The Principle

Everyone is a prospect. Wealth can be easily overlooked because of false assumptions. The book *The Millionaire Next Door* demonstrates this truth. Genuine wealth is not always apparent. Some of the fun of philanthropy is derived from finding giving potential where others have not.

The Story

For many years Miss Flood taught piano lessons for 35¢ an hour. Upon her death, she left more than $1 million to a local hospital for cancer research. She would never have shown up on a typical prospect list.

Melvin worked for the phone company all his life. He had installed phones in more than 30,000 homes during his long career. This in-house experience enabled him on several occasions to see first-hand the valuable support and encouragement seeing eye dogs gave to the visually impaired. As a result, he gave more than $1 million to the local seeing eye dog association.

Don was a manufacturers' representative, and Mildred taught piano lessons. They lived an unassuming lifestyle in a modest home in an unpretentious neighborhood. During their lifetime they gave several million dollars and when they died, their entire estate, to a local community college.

The Lesson

View everyone as a prospective donor. Research to unearth hidden treasure in relationships and philanthropy. Discovering the "millionaires next door" can be a challenge, but the greater challenge is to find a way to connect these people to your institution or agency.

Welcome The Donor's Objections

The Principle

No one likes to be criticized or told they have failed to do something well, yet this kind of feedback is crucial to improving effectiveness. When a donor does not volunteer dissatisfaction, there is no opportunity to correct the problem.

The Story

Renee's family had established a major foundation that supported a number of causes at a university. At her first meeting with Jim, a fund raiser for the university, she said, "You know, Jim, I like you. But there are some people I do not necessarily like. I am going to give you a list of everyone I do not want to sit with, have lunch with, or even see on my trips back to the university." Clearly Renee had experienced an unpleasant visit in the past and wanted to make sure that future trips were positive. Jim tentatively took down the names.

Unfortunately, the university's president was among them. This created an awkward situation. Jim explained to Renee that avoiding the president would not be easy. "Minimize the contact," she answered. Jim got the message and the gift for the university as well. Renee and her foundation made several gifts over the years, including endowing a chair for more than $1 million. Before she died, Renee expressed to Jim her appreciation for the attention he had given her preferences.

The Lesson

If the donor has a concern, listen. Even though the effort to meet an objection may be difficult, the fund raiser's role is to help donors make gifts. Objections are opportunities in disguise.

Bring Your Projects To Life

The Principle

In trying to communicate the value of an institution, a fund raiser may exhaust all possible superlatives: "greatest" agency, "superior" institution, "highest quality" students, "best" care for residents, and "finest" medical facility.

But even a trustworthy fund raiser's interpretation of the agency's value is best substantiated through real-life examples. Stories with texture and weight allow the quality of the institution to speak for itself. Like faux leather or synthetic silk, anything less than reality misses the mark.

The Story

Lisa was in charge of a large adoption agency, and she was very much in her niche. She understood the agency well. She had founded it and served as executive director for more than a decade.

Lisa was trying to persuade her board to move forward with a $1.5 million capital campaign. To support her case, Lisa shared the story of 11 year-old Kelly. After years of foster care and the termination of parental rights, she was referred to the adoption agency. In conversations with her counselor, Kelly expressed doubts that she would ever be adopted. She knew that most adoptive parents preferred to adopt newborns or younger children. The counselor reassured Kelly and affirmed how special she really was.

The agency periodically held picnics for potential adoptive parents, couples who had already adopted children, and a number of children who were available for adoption. Kelly decided to market herself, believing this might be her last chance for a "normal" family life. She put on her best dress, the one with the lovely red flower, and spent extra time fixing her hair.

As the guests arrived, Kelly approached each and every couple asking if they were interested in adoption. One couple in particular caught Kelly's eye and she asked, "What age child are you planning to adopt?" They told her they were thinking of someone around eleven. "I'm eleven," she offered. They visited for a while and the couple moved on. Encouraged, Kelly was determined to do everything she could to make a good impression on this couple.

Later, Kelly asked them if they had decided on anyone. "No," they responded, "but we're still thinking about it."

"Are you thinking about me?" she asked.

"Yes, Kelly, we are," they told her.

"So you won't forget me?" she implored.

"No, we won't forget you, Kelly," the couple assured her.

The agency had created a picture board of potential adoptees for this occasion. Kelly ran to the board, took down her picture and ran out to the car as the couple prepared to leave. She knocked on the car window, and as they lowered it, she handed them the photo. "Here is my picture, so you won't forget me," she told them. They assured her that she would not be forgotten—and she wasn't. Three weeks later the couple adopted Kelly.

Needless to say, the board voted unanimously to move forward with the campaign.

The Lesson

Real stories demonstrate the impact of a gift far more effectively than a fund raiser's most complimentary presentation. Do not overlook the human implications of fund-raising. Kelly's story certainly illustrates the impact of philanthropy.

Bring along examples that are rich with the stories, places, feelings and faces of real people who have been helped.

Who's Minding The Store?

The Principle

When developing a plan for solicitation, look for positive relationships between the prospective donors and agency staff. Capitalize on people who are available, rather than trying to do it all yourself. Ask around. Which people make donors feel the most comfortable? It might be Jack, the social worker, or Mary, the counselor. It could be Bill, the development officer, or Newton, the chief financial officer. Perhaps it is Charles, the executive director, Charlotte, the program director, or even John and Mary, who serve as houseparents.

Expand your viewpoint beyond the horizons of the typical fund raiser and consider those who have their fingers on an agency's pulse. Donors feel comfortable with people who are not trying to impress them. They feel comfortable with people who are really sold on the agency. Donors want the people actually involved in the agency's work to know about their gifts. Camaraderie in fund raising, rather than a sense of competition, makes donors more inclined to give.

The Story

The Salvation Army had been receiving a number of gifts from a local businessman Anthony and his family. His family's wealth was generated from a toy manufacturing company and related subsidiary companies.

The Salvation Army was in the middle of a Christmas kettle drive as well as a capital campaign. The chief fund raiser, Christine, was anxious for the opportunity to solicit Anthony for a significant gift to the effort. Christine had placed numerous calls to Anthony most of which were returned by Anthony's assistant. Obviously, Anthony was a very busy man and not able to attend many events or special occasions. Christine believed Anthony was a difficult if not impossible man to reach.

As the Salvation Army prepared for the annual Christmas dinner, Anthony returned one of Christine's calls. Christine was out of the office preparing for the event that evening, so Anthony spoke with Christine's assistant, Denise. Denise, who had been with the Salvation Army for many years and was very familiar with the dynamics of the development office, knew that Christine was anxious to visit with Anthony and how difficult it was to reach him. Denise had developed a great dedication for her work on the campaign and was an excellent spokesperson. After a brief exchange regarding the status of the Christmas appeal, she took a chance and invited Anthony to come to the dinner that night and hand out his company's toys to the children and their families.

Fortunately, Anthony and his entire family were able to attend the event. They had a wonderful time handing out their toys and meeting the people who worked for and were served by the Salvation Army. They were captivated by the real life stories being told and were able to learn firsthand how their money was helping.

The next day Christine got a call from Anthony at home. He was interested in discussing how he and his family might help the capital campaign.

The Lesson

Take note of those in an agency who best characterize its intent and aspirations, who accurately represent the vitality of the institution and allow donors to feel most at ease. Involve these people in the solicitation process. When met with true enthusiasm and commitment, a donor finds it hard to say no.

Respect The Short-term Perspective

The Principle

Small business owners and professionals, such as doctors, lawyers, or accountants, often cannot project the short or long-range success of their business with confidence. Give these prospective donors maximum levels of control in determining the size and distribution schedule of their gifts.

The Story

Marvin was a successful businessman. Each year Gretchen, a fund raiser, asked him how business was progressing and what Marvin projected for the future. He would answer good-naturedly, "You know, I just don't know what is going to happen six months from now." Marvin wanted to be a philanthropist, but this short-term view had always been too great a stumbling block for other fund raisers.

Gretchen realized that gifts solicited from Marvin would have to take into account his short-term view of his financial prospects. She arranged for Marvin to give $1 million within a five-year period, allowing Marvin to choose the amounts and the times of the payments. This respected his short-term perspective, and he donated the full amount before the five years had passed.

The Lesson

To some degree, being wary of long-term financial commitments allows flexibility that keeps small businesses solvent. These professionals never take the future for granted. Most prepare a "six-month crisis" plan so that if everything goes wrong for six months, they know they have the resources to manage.

Knowing this tendency, fund raisers can develop strategies to give donors maximum flexibility. Donors should feel confident that they will be able to meet their commitments and still weather a worst-case, six-month crisis.

Won't You be My Neighbor?

The Principle

The ability to uncover prospects that others have overlooked calls for a combination of opportunity, creativity, and tenacity. A fund raiser must first expect to find these individuals, approaching prospect identification with an explorers sense of anticipation and adventure. This expectancy is not an assumed attitude to put a fund raiser in the correct frame of mind. It is the difference between an average fund raiser and an extraordinary one. An outstanding fund raiser knows the donors are out there, and her job is to find them. This perspective generates the creativity necessary to locate and encourage a valuable donor relationship.

One way to discover donors that others may have overlooked is to determine who owns property or occupies buildings within a block radius of the agency's property. These owners and tenants often have insights into the function and public image of the agency. Even if they have never met any of the agency's staff, these neighbors typically have an impression of the agency based on proximity and daily observation.

The Story

Gerald was a neighbor of an agency for children with disabilities. He and his wife were unable to have children of their own, but for 40 years they had enjoyed the children's caroling at Christmas and trick-or-treating at Halloween. Shortly after Gerald's wife passed away and not long before his 75th birthday, he was invited to a neighborhood appreciation party at the agency. Gerald indicated at that party that he had never been invited to the agency before.

Robert, who was knowledgeable in real estate, recognized Gerald as having been an appraiser who had acquired more than a modest sum of money in his lifetime. Robert considered Gerald a likely donor prospect, and Gerald eventually donated more than $1 million to the agency.

Gerald not only provided monetary support, but served as a mentor to the children, offered special awards for their efforts and attended all the agency special events. He became a real part of the agency.

Toward the end of Gerald's life, he shared that because of his relationship with the agency, his last years had been full of purpose and meaning.

The Lesson

Get to know your neighbors. These people already know more about your agency than you realize. Cultivate these relationships.

Remember Special Days

The Principle

Cultivation is critical to the overall success of a solicitation. An important element of cultivating good donor relations is remembering events special to a donor—birthdays, anniversaries, holidays, and others. It is the "others" that can set an organization apart.

Most fund-raising organizations are going to remember the obvious special days—the birthdays and the anniversaries. But it is possibly even more important to remember the special days that highlight the relationship between the donor and the institution.

For example, the date of the donor's first contribution could become an anniversary of sorts, or the day their major gift was announced. What matters is that it best represents the relationship between that donor and the institution. Looking at the relationship in a special way strengthens the connection.

The Story

Dean made his first major gift to a museum on Valentine's Day. His million-dollar gift gave the museum the working capital to acquire works of art when the opportunity arose. The fund eventually became known informally as the Valentine's Day Acquisition Fund.

To commemorate this gift, each year the museum's director, Neil, sent out a special Valentine's Day remembrance to all patrons of the museum over the age of 80. Nearly all were women. This remembrance of Valentine's Day was one of the few if not the only Valentine's Day sentiments these individuals would receive. One patron, Gail, was so touched by this gesture that she gave a significant gift to the Valentine's Day Acquisition Fund and has continued to do so each Valentine's Day.

The Lesson

Donors, like everyone else, want to be recognized as special and unique. Remember them individually and relish the relationship.

Solicit IPO Stockholders

The Principle

Most gifts are not given by corporations or foundations, but by individuals. For growing companies, giving a substantial gift can directly affect the value of the company's stock. When deciding to purchase stock in a company, many investors use a cash-to-debt ratio to determine soundness. Any reduction in cash might appear as a loss of profitability, which may diminish the value of the stock.

For this reason, emerging companies are reluctant to alter the financial statement by giving away large sums of money. On the other hand, those profiting from the growth of a company—the owners of the Initial Public Offering (IPO) stock—are in a position to give amazing gifts to worthwhile projects.

The Story

Recently, the owners of the company responsible for the Yahoo! search engine gave $2 million to their alma mater. That gift came from them personally, not from the company.

Given the level of growth that many companies are experiencing, owners of these stocks can literally grow back their money in a short period of time while taking the capital gains tax advantages of donating appreciated stock.

The Lesson

Look beyond the large corporations and think in terms of individual gifts. With many new companies emerging, owners of IPO stocks represent great opportunities.

Many Gifts Don't Appear on Tax Returns

The Principle

Some gifts made to nonprofit organizations never show up as deductions on income tax returns. Many smaller gifts do not reach thresholds established by tax criteria. At other times, anonymity is so important to donors that they are unwilling to even list their gifts on tax forms.

The opportunity to receive a tax deduction for a gift is rare in the field of philanthropy worldwide. The idea of giving to those in need is unique in this country. Most other cultures do not understand philanthropy.

This is not to say that deductions should not be fully utilized. They should not, however, be considered the central selling point.

The Story

People in the Midwest say, "When your neighbor's barn burns, you don't wait to see if you can get a tax deduction to build them a new one." In today's society, many barns are burning. Neighbors need help and gifts of many levels are extended without any type of recognition from the IRS or elsewhere.

Fund raisers often ponder why some organizations manage to get the gift and others do not. Do the most important organizations get more money? No. Is one more vital than the other? No way! The major reason some organizations get more gifts is due to the way they handle those gifts.

In addition to tax considerations, people respond positively to requests for money because:

1. You ask them to give.
2. They know their gifts will make a difference.
3. They know their gifts will have an impact.
4. You recognize them for their gifts.
5. You enable them to gain personal connections with other individuals who are passionately involved in some meaningful dimension of life.
6. You allow them to get back at the corrupt or unjust.
7. They have the discretionary wealth to give it away.
8. They feel it's their duty.
9. You allow them to relieve guilt about any ethical, political, or personal transgression, real or imagined.
10. You enable them to do something about a major problem or issue.
11. You enable them to offer opinions and share their attitudes.
12. You help them learn about a complex and interesting problem or issue.
13. They are afraid the project will fail without them.
14. You give them the chance to release emotional tension caused by a life-threatening situation, a critical emergency or an ethical dilemma.
15. They believe it is a blessing to do so.
16. You give them a chance to be associated with a famous or worthy person.
17. You give them the opportunity to belong to something as a member, friend or supporter.
18. You give them something tangible in return.
19. They have a philanthropic habit.
20. You help them preserve their world view by validating cherished values and beliefs.
21. They have demonstrated that they support organizations like yours.
22. They know their gifts will accomplish something right now.

23. You appreciate them for their gifts.
24. You acknowledge the values they express in their giving.
25. You encourage them to change people's lives with their gifts.
26. You highlight their worthiness.
27. Others they respect have given and invite them to make a gift.
28. You aid them in doing something for a family member, a friend, a child or grandchild.
29. You show them a way to make a gift and get a personal return.
30. They can help achieve a goal.
31. They can express personal gratitude for something that helped them or their family.
32. They can honor personal achievement.
33. They can focus attention on an agency with which they identify.
34. You have made it easy to make a gift by offering pledge payments or credit cards.
35. You have been thorough in your presentation and they can't see a reason not to give.
36. They respect the leaders of the organization.
37. You tell the truth.
38. You listen to their needs and ambitions.
39. You give the donor more than she expects.
40. You don't argue.
41. You return phone calls.
42. You have every detail of your proposal well in hand.
43. You don't apply too much pressure to give.
44. You develop a relationship with the donor that enhances confidence.
45. You enjoy yourself in the fund-raising work, and others can see that.
46. You seek the donor's advice on particular aspects of the projects need.
47. You involve the donor's family or company in the project.
48. You speak clearly and confidently.
49. You know the importance of the donor's time and you use it wisely.
50. Your appearance is professional and appropriate.
51. You are creative in finding ways for the donor to make the gift.
52. Your approach to the project is creative and unique.

53. You position your donor as your mentor or a mentor to others in the organization.
54. You say thanks in informal ways that get the donor's attention.
55. You tell others of the donor's gift and how he or she has made a difference.
56. Your donor knows you work hard and give all you can to the agency.
57. You deal with people as people, not as things.
58. You don't garner all the glory, but share success with others in the organization.
59. You know someone has touched that person's life in a dramatic way.
60. You critically evaluate yourself.
61. You are persistent in your solicitation of the gift.
62. You don't blame others when you are at fault.
63. Your agency or institution works as a team.
64. Your ego has not outdistanced your message.
65. You follow up after a request has been made.
66. You are not discouraged easily.
67. When you are told no, you listen to see if you can learn from this temporary setback.
68. You are consistent in the themes of your presentations.
69. You think of the group or organization first and yourself second.
70. Your agency is focused on its mission and is not trying to be all things to all people.
71. You don't procrastinate on calling prospects and donors.
72. You respond promptly to questions asked by your donor.
73. You establish a personal bond with the prospect.
74. The donor is inspired by the potential of the project.
75. The integrity of the organization strengthens the donor's confidence.
76. The agency pays its bills on time.

The Lesson

For a few donors, the tax deduction is the driving force behind their giving. However, given that these donors can choose to give to thousands of different nonprofit organizations, their thoughts usually focus on non-tax considerations first.

Do not lead your solicitation requests with the advantages of tax deductions. Instead, lead with a project that interests the donor through which the donor can change lives. Then provide an opportunity to maximize the tax advantages of the donation.

Money In Motion Creates Opportunity

The Principle

When a business is bought or sold, money is in motion. When a couple is married or divorced, money is in motion. When a trust fund, a retirement fund, or a prenuptial agreement is established, money is in motion. When an inheritance is received, money is in motion. Money that is moved around rapidly is apt to "spill."

Fund raisers should be on the alert for money in motion.

The Story

Wendell owned a bank that had an employee stock option plan (ESOP). He wanted to make a gift to an important hospital project, and he also needed to move substantial funds into his company's ESOP. Given these considerations, Larry, the hospital's development officer, suggested that Wendell donate a gift of stock to the hospital, then have his company's ESOP buy the stock out of the hospital's hands.

Larry funded his ESOP while also fulfilling his commitment to the hospital. His million-dollar gift to the agency cost him only a few hundred thousand dollars.

The Lesson

When a donor's money is in motion—or about to move—be ready to suggest how that movement could benefit the donor's philanthropic interests.

Watch for Life-Changing Events

The Principle

People are more inclined to consider estate planning at significant crossroads in life. When a profound event occurs—birth, death, marriage, divorce, job change, relocation, or even distant travel (especially overseas)—it interrupts the ordinary. The routines of daily life drown out thoughts of planning for the unexpected. These changes awaken an awareness of mortality that can prompt people to arrange a legacy for the future. A fund raiser needs to be aware of these windows of opportunity. The need to be remembered is fundamental. For many, estate planning is a tangible way to address this need. Deferred gifts can be included among other estate-planning options.

The Story

Joan was not able to attend college, but recognized the importance of higher education and the significant impact women in the work force could have on society. When Joan became ill with mild symptoms of multiple sclerosis, she decided to create a $5,000 scholarship to honor women who wanted to re-enter the work force. While discussing this gift with development professionals, Joan mentioned that she was reviewing her estate plan. She and her husband were traveling to Australia soon and, because she was not well-traveled, she was apprehensive about going overseas. The trip prompted her to put her financial affairs in order.

In the process of considering her estate, Joan added a $30,000 trust to the $5,000 scholarship. A few days later, Joan added a $100,000 separate bequest, and subsequently an additional $500,000 bequest to fund this scholarship. If Joan had not been reviewing her estate plan, the opportunity for including those elements in her estate could have been lost.

The Lesson

Watch for potentially life-changing events. When they occur, be available to assist the donor.

Estates Shape Million-Dollar Commitments

The Principle

Planned giving creates anxiety in the minds of many fund raisers. Some fund raisers may not grasp the technicalities of the process while others may think donors will be turned off by the discussion of death-related gifts. However, this form of giving should be one of the important tools of choice of any good development officer.

By definition, planned giving is a method by which an individual commits to a nonprofit a certain portion of his financial assets, generally allocated upon the donor's death. Frequently, planned giving can use the assets for the lifetime benefit of the donor with the balance ultimately going to an institution.

Planned giving has become an important strategic element of most million-dollar gifts. The result is that a fund raiser wanting to secure a million-dollar gift needs to have mastered the details of planned gift options.

The Story

Michael, the husband of an important political leader, decided that it was the appropriate time for his wife Dollie to be publicly honored in her community and state. At the time, renovations were under way to turn the multipurpose area of an old civic facility into a recreation center. The campaign committee organized a special gift opportunity for the naming of the center. To obtain the honor of choosing the center's name, it was agreed that a donor would need to give $1 million.

Michael felt that Dollie should receive recognition for her years of service and saw the center-naming opportunity as an ideal way to achieve this. He made an overture to the campaign regarding his interest. The campaign organizers visited with this couple and were offered a $200,000 single-check cash donation. The fund raisers politely clarified the need for the full $1 million for the honor of naming the center.

The couple then reviewed their assets and singled out a $500,000 tract of land that was not producing enough income to impact their quality of life. They offered to increase their gift to include the land. With their gift now at $700,000, Michael again requested the opportunity to name the center. Although the agency was still unable to comply for a gift of less than $1 million, an alternative method was offered.

The agency suggested that if Michael and Dollie provided for the remaining $300,000 in their estate plan, they could secure the naming opportunity. A contract against the will was executed for $300,000, and the center is now named for Dollie. Michael and Dollie were grateful to be able to assemble their gift from a variety of assets.

The Lesson

When developing a gift plan, especially for a major gift of $1 million or more, consider the donors' assets and think about what can be put together in order for them to reach the highest gift-giving level possible.

In this case, three kinds of gifts were used: cash, land (which was converted to cash after the gift), and a planned gift (which would be received posthumously).

The fear that fund raisers sometimes have towards planned gifts often relates to the technical aspects of estate planning. When considering planned gifts, fund raisers should continue to focus on the giving, not the planning. People enjoy giving because they feel that they have the resources to give and because they believe in the institution. It is up to estate-planning professionals to help the prospective donor determine the proper vehicle to achieve the desired giving level.

Inter-Faith Ministries

Fund-Raising Fears No More

The organizers of Inter-Faith Ministries (IFM) in Wichita, Kansas, learned an important lesson in fund raising: people do not give simply because you have a need. In the past, the leadership at Inter-Faith Ministries operated on the assumption that being strapped for funds was simply part of nonprofit life. Each time they came face to face with another financial crisis they made another appeal for funds. For years, their reactionary method of fund raising worked, but over time it did not prove to be reliable.

In recent years, however, Inter-Faith Ministries' Executive Director, Sam Muyskens, says he and his fellow organizers realized that "crisis" fund raising was no longer acceptable. They knew they had to become proactive.

Inter-Faith Ministries' mission is to "build inter-religious under-standing, promote justice, relieve misery and reconcile the estranged . . . offer hope, healing and understanding." Participating within the structure of Inter-Faith Ministries are Jewish, Protestant, Roman Catholic, Muslim, Buddhist, Baha'i and Unitarian Universalists communities. Inter-Faith Ministries strives to meet basic human needs such as food, shelter, medical care and education. The group provides homeless services to individuals who do not fit into the service categories of other agencies. They offer continuous case management for all residents, a resident assistant program with a continuum of care for individuals who show a desire to work, and a follow-up program for up to two years after residents leave the shelter.

While Inter-Faith Ministries was a highly visible and integral part of the Wichita community, the organization literally survived on a wing and a prayer. Despite their efforts, they found themselves faced with a deficit of more than $100,000. After hiring a development director, things gradually began to turn around, but they could not count on government dollars—HUD monies were no longer available. Traditional congregations and other ecumenical/interfaith organizations were also having financial difficulties.

As funds proved scarce, Inter-Faith became determined to succeed. What began as a campaign goal of $1 million eventually became a multi-stage fund drive which now has produced more than $3 million, as well as the acquisition of three buildings.

How to Ask Is as Important as Why

The key ingredients, Muyskens says, were a strong belief in the organization, pride in the programs offered and compassion for the people served. He says they eventually determined that how they asked for funds was as important as why they asked.

"We knew we had to look at something different," says Muyskens. "Three years ago our board met and decided we would try something big. We interviewed political and religious leaders to find out how we were viewed in the community and found that people thought of us as a program of dignity, but one that was always in financial difficulty."

Selection of a Strategy

"At that point," continues Muyskens, "we had a board retreat and determined that we needed to think bigger. We put together a wish list which came down to four key elements: create a program and ministry center, build a homeless shelter, erase our debt, and provide an endowment."

After presenting their plans to Inter-Faith Ministries' governing board, the decision was made to retain the services of a fund-raising consultant to help them realize their financial goals. The consultant recommended that we not begin actively seeking funds until we had completed a preliminary campaign assessment to help us determine exactly where we were headed."

Setting a Goal

The actual fund raising got under way with a gift from a board member who agreed to pay for the study. Results of that study suggested that Inter-Faith Ministries set a goal to raise $1 million and gear it toward underwriting the homeless shelter, setting up the endowment and erasing the debt.

"We decided to put the program center on the back burner, and look to a program security fund, primarily underwritten by board members, to erase the program debt," Muyskens says.

Throughout the process, what initially seemed to be setbacks often brought forth new opportunities. During their search for a 5,000-square foot building to call home, Inter-Faith Ministries leaders stumbled on a structure which offered 13,500 square feet. While it was perfect for their needs, they knew that realistically it would take at least a $350,000 contribution for them to acquire the property. Their real estate agent helped identify a person with a possible interest in providing the funds.

"We applied for and received State of Kansas tax credits and were awarded a $350,000 contribution towards the campaign," Muyskens says. "When that gift became a reality, our $1 million campaign goal grew to $1.6 million and included a program and ministry center."

Major Gifts

Prior to receiving the $350,000 building gift, Inter-Faith Ministries received a $200,000 challenge gift from a long-time contributor. Local corporations and foundations stepped forward with needed gifts. Included were Builders, Inc., which gave $90,000 for the shelter, $75,000 from Cessna Foundation for the shelter elevator, $50,000 from the W.T. Kemper Foundation, $30,000 from Western Resources and many others.

"A couple of major gifts help give credibility to an organization," Muyskens says. "We found that visiting with the local businesses and organizations was paying off. We were able to get close to the 50 percent mark and then received a Mabee Foundation challenge grant. The Mabee Foundation in Tulsa, Oklahoma, supports regional construction projects. After receiving estimates for the necessary renovations, we found that we needed a little more and raised the goal to $1.9 million."

Though their mission remained constant, plans and goals changed throughout the campaign. Inter-Faith Ministries had not originally intended to put new heating and air conditioning into the shelter. A donor decided that he would like to add those comforts to both buildings, which meant a $110,000 contribution from him, but this created an additional $50,000 expense, which totaled $160,000.

"We discovered that when we asked, people responded," Muyskens says. "Over a period of time we got to 80 percent of our goal and eventually announced the campaign at $2 million." Ivonne Goldstein, Wichita community leader, and Don Barry, vice president of A.G. Edwards, served as campaign co-chairs. John Himmell, chairman, Commerce Bank and Bill Moore, president, KGE (the local utility company), were secured for the roles of honorary campaign chairs.

A Second Campaign

Previously, Inter-Faith had responded to a city homeless coalition which asked them to create a safe haven for the chronically, mentally ill homeless.

"We wrote a grant, but it was denied," Muyskens says. "A year later we re-submitted a grant and just forgot about it and did not include Safe Haven in the original campaign. Subsequently, the grant was accepted creating the need to raise another $600,000 to make the Safe Haven work."

Organizers took this proposal back to the board and suggested a second campaign geared specifically toward raising funds for Safe Haven. They found several potential buildings, but none fit their budget. Then they learned that the clinic across the street from Inter-Faith Ministries' program and ministries center had moved to another location.

"An elderly woman owned it. Our consultant recommended that we make her an offer using a planned gift approach," Muyskens explains. "We asked if she would be interested in a charitable gift annuity. Five years of lease payments were bought out by the lessee, which helped provide moneys for the annuity. It was a win/win situation. Additional dollars were raised to purchase an annuity that would guarantee the donor an income and ensure her security. Her gift was valued at $365,000."

At this point, Inter-Faith Ministries had two campaigns going. They were in the final stages of the capital campaign, going out to the donor base and the community. The second campaign to establish Safe Haven for the mentally ill homeless community was emerging with a $2.5 million goal.

"By April 1998, we had gone over the $2 million mark and declared victory for the initial campaign," Muyskens says. That campaign was closed out with a special community campaign called Heart to Heart, which commemorated Inter-Faith Ministries' 112 years of service. This campaign attracted more than $22,000 in gifts from over 100 donors. Ms. Goldstein served as the chair for this special closing effort.

"As a fund raiser and volunteer for Inter-Faith Ministries, we gained much from our consultant," Ms. Goldstein says, "In a short time, we dramatically expanded and matured in our fund-raising efforts. These efforts will provide more and better community services for our specialized program."

What Did We Learn?

Muyskens says he found it helpful to be accountable to consultants on a regular basis. This worked to keep the campaign more focused and productive. Additionally, he learned some creative planned-giving strategies. Though he never considered himself a fund raiser, he now has different ideas about the process as well as a little more faith in himself.

"I discovered that fund raising was not such a daunting task. I am no longer inhibited its intricacies. I am proud of what I have accomplished at Inter-Faith Ministries and believe wholeheartedly in our mission. Often our prospects feel honored to be asked to serve or provide other support. I have also learned that 'no' is not always negative and should not be taken personally. Sometimes 'no' can become 'yes.' I am never offended when I am told no. I have learned that not everyone can give at the moment they are asked."

According to Muyskens, some of the smaller contributions were the biggest surprises. "A person whom I've always considered a friend saw that we were putting in an elevator and sent $5,000 toward renovation expenses. The relationships that we have built in the community are very gratifying."

His own view of Inter-Faith Ministries also has changed.

"I have a new vision of the role Inter-Faith Ministries can play within the community," says Muyskens. "This campaign has generated many ideas about what Inter-Faith Ministries can do for the community such as decreasing violence, perpetuating equality for all people, and nurturing children's physical and spiritual health. We can address all of these issues if the community works together. We must think big to accomplish these objectives."

Thank You. . .
Thank You. . .
And by the Way,
Thank You!

Stewardship Is More Than Sending A Receipt

The Principle

Besides the legal obligation to acknowledge a donation with a receipt, the receipt confirms that the agency received a specific amount of money which was not exchanged for any goods or services. Stewardship, however, means a great deal more. Good stewardship involves trust and integrity. It means following through with promises and ensuring that the gift is used in accordance with the donor's intent.

To accomplish this consistently, an agency must adopt a gift stewardship policy. The following is an example of such a policy.

It is the intention of the XYZ Organization to be good stewards of the gifts provided for the benefit of the XYZ Organization. To that end, the board will give strict attention to its fiduciary responsibility to provide conservative, strong and consistent management of all funds entrusted to it, in accordance with the "prudent person" investment standard.

Acceptance of all gifts by the XYZ Organization's staff will be in accordance with the Gift Acceptance Policy. Emphasis shall be placed on preserving the value of each gift; therefore, all gifts, with the exception of life insurance and annuity products, shall be converted to cash in an orderly fashion. Informed professionals may be used to assist in the disposal of items requiring specialized knowledge. Pending utilization for the purpose for which given, the net cash proceeds from all gifts, along with gifts of cash, shall, unless otherwise required by the donor, be invested in accordance with the XYZ Organization's Investment Policy, having the safeguarding of principal as the primary objective.

All gifts will be utilized only for those purposes identified by the donor and will be recognized as described by the donor of the funds, pursuant to the Gift Recognition Policy.

For investment purposes, the proceeds of gifts may be commingled and grouped together with other monies. The handling of gifts shall be reviewed at least quarterly by the XYZ Organization's board to ensure compliance with the purpose designated by the donor.

The XYZ Organization's staff shall publish annually a report on fund activities. This report will be distributed to the board and be available to donors and other designated persons upon request.

A stewardship policy indicates that an agency will remain in communication with the donor regarding the use of the gift. If asked, the agency will be able to verify that the gift is being used in accordance with the donor's desire. This kind of methodical conscientiousness builds the donor's confidence and protects the potential for future gifts.

The Story

Six months after Clark gave $10,000 to a private school, he had not received a letter of thanks and was still waiting on a tax receipt to verify the gift. Clark finally received the receipt by the end of the calendar year but only after repeated requests to the business office.

When confronted with the lack of good stewardship reflected by this incident, the headmaster countered by saying, "Ten thousand dollars was not much money for this guy. He really should have given more." His response was shocking and unfortunate.

Without saying a word to the donor, the headmaster made clear his feelings: this gift was not valued.

Although the headmaster may not have realized it, Clark interpreted this lack of acknowledgment as an indication that the school did not really need the gift. As a result, he decided that future giving to the school was unnecessary. Why give where it was not needed? Not surprisingly, Clark designated his future gifts to another institution that did acknowledge and value his gifts.

The Lesson

Every gift, regardless of size, should be acknowledged promptly, appreciated graciously, and valued sincerely. Ungratefulness is guaranteed to fail.

Make Every Donor Happy Every Day

The Principle

In order to ensure that donors are happy, fund raisers must make them feel cared for, trusted and admired. The donor must believe that the fund raiser wants to offer support whenever possible. Consider current donors every day, particularly those who have given major gifts. Think of ways to help them be successful. Let them know that their gifts have a tremendous, positive influence.

The Story

Ralph and Francine made a multi-million-dollar gift to their alma mater. Eric, the vice president of development, communicated regularly with Ralph and Francine but did not give them inordinate attention.

Ralph's daughter, Shelly, wanted to gain admittance into the MBA program at the college, but she was having trouble with the entrance exams. Because Ralph did not want to misuse his position or wealth, he did not make any calls or push open any doors on Shelly's behalf, nor did Shelly want any special treatment. Her grades were solid, but her struggle with taking tests impeded her progress.

Everyone knew Shelly was Ralph's daughter although she made no effort to make it known. Aware of Shelly's struggle, Eric went to the dean of the business school and discovered that there was a provision for students in these circumstances to be admitted on a probationary basis. This was not an unusual procedure, and the dean felt it would be appropriate for Shelly. Eric suggested that the dean contact Shelly with this information without mentioning their meeting. The dean agreed to make the call. Shelly was not admitted immediately, as it was still necessary to fulfill the requirements for this particular procedure, but it made her aware of an opportunity that she had not known was available.

Eric did not tell Shelly or Ralph about his extra effort to uncover this information. Eric's goal was not to get around any regulations or bend any rules. He was not even interested in taking bows for his contribution. His motivation was to make life easier for Ralph. He had the donor's best interest at heart.

The Lesson

Take every appropriate step to maximize the donor's access to available help, encouragement and support. Every day, consider ways to advance the donor's cause. Remove roadblocks, expedite efforts and simplify complications to make things smoother and more enjoyable for the donor. Selfless actions will be repaid a hundredfold.

"Front-Door" Fund Raisers

The Principle

The first impression of an agency often comes from the receptionist. This person is often the first to greet visitors and makes many contacts by phone, creating first impressions that are hard to erase. Agencies benefit from having interested, congenial, helpful people serve in those front positions.

The Story

Juanita had been the receptionist for a homeless ministry for many years. In that time, she had opportunities to become the office manager or the secretary to the director. Each time, however, she chose to continue to work with the public. She felt that she could be of more service to the agency by providing a good first impression than she could by working behind the scenes.

Juanita was sensitive to those needing assistance with housing and related issues. She had a clear understanding of the program and could answer donor questions with intelligence and professionalism. Overall, she had become indispensable in her current position, and she knew the value of her contribution. Although she would be the last to say so, her efforts had an enormous impact on individual lives as well as the agency.

Brian, a donor who had supported the work of the ministry for a while, called in to ask some questions and spoke at length with Juanita. She conveyed to Brian the excitement of seeing people being given a second chance and helped in remarkable ways. On another occasion, she described how discouraging it was to see needs unmet and hopes unrealized. Through their many conversations, she gave him a good picture of the work this ministry was doing.

One day, Brian showed up in person for the first time. As usual, Juanita greeted the guest and began a conversation. Her first impression was that this might be someone in need of the agency's assistance. Before long, though, she realized this was Brian. Brian had been a farmer for many years and had accumulated wealth through hard work and wise management. He also had a big heart. He let Juanita know that the reason for his visit was to drop off a check for the work of the ministry. Excited to hear this, Juanita was ready to get the executive director. Brian stopped her. "No, Juanita," he replied, "Norton is doing a fine job for the shelter, and I appreciate his work, but this gift is being given in honor of your work. You are the front door to the agency, and you are a good one. Thank you for being such a fine representative." The check was for $2 million.

The Lesson

The "front-door" employees of an agency create that all-important first impression. Make sure that the highest quality people are right where they should be—at the front.

Thank The Donor "Seven Times"

The Principle

The golden rule of fund raising is "Thank the donor seven times before asking for the next gift." Despite years of repetition, this axiom has not lost its importance. The donor must feel genuinely appreciated before it is ever appropriate or prudent to ask for an additional gift.

Rather than a literal number, "seven times" suggests the completeness of showing thanks. For some, this may require many more than seven overtures of thankfulness, specific to the giver and to the particular situation. For others, a smaller number of very personalized thanks will demonstrate the agency's gratitude.

The Story

At a training seminar on solicitation, this axiom was shared with a group of fund-raising professionals. Among the attendees was a young, enthusiastic fund raiser, Arnold, who was eager to learn and to follow all the available advice. His talent, attitude and energy were admirable, and he had a sincere commitment to his college. This commitment and strong belief in his work motivated him to be aggressive in accomplishing his goals. Upon completing the seminar, this young man was eager to get out and apply the newly acquired principles.

Chris, the chairman of the board of Arnold's community college, was also an acquaintance of the fund-raising speaker. Chris called the speaker, wondering about some of the young fund raiser's strategies. "Arnold has just raised $100,000 from one of our donors," he said. "This is the largest gift our community college has ever received. We're really very excited about it, but there's something I don't understand. He sent the donor a thank you letter, and he asked five other trustees to write and thank her also. Now he's very anxious for me to send my letter because he wants to go back and solicit her again. I'm a little uncomfortable with this plan because it doesn't seem that enough time has elapsed for another solicitation."

Obviously, the rule-of-thumb became a math formula for Arnold. One thank-you letter from him, plus five from the trustees, plus one from Chris equaled seven thank yous and another solicitation. Perhaps Arnold thought his whole budget could be raised this way—thank her seven times and head back over.

The Lesson

Donor recognition and attention given after the fact is sometimes viewed as a time-consuming chore. But thanking a donor allows a fund raiser to focus on the sacrifice the donor has made. Regardless of the amount given (or the amount the donor has left), it is important to remember that she could have chosen a multitude of other ways to use it. Instead, she gave to a specific organization she felt would accomplish work she believed in.

Thanking a donor should come as naturally as breathing, but until it becomes second nature, a fund raiser must not give thanks in a perfunctory way, but in a complete way—"seven times."

Value the Donor's Gift

The Principle

The value of a gift extends beyond its dollar amount. The real value comes from what it can do. As donors see how their money is changing people's lives, they feel that they have invested their money, not merely given it away.

This can be most effectively affirmed by those without direct association to the agency. When an outsider shows that the gift is valued, the donor is made especially aware of its impact. By selectively encouraging expressions of appreciation from others in the community, an agency demonstrates that the donor's gift was recognized as important.

The Story

Walter and June made a gift of $7 million to fund a new building on their alma mater's campus. This couple was civic minded, and had contributed to many nonprofits within the community. As a result of their generosity, they had received many and varying forms of recognition. Warren, the vice president for advancement, knew he would need to find a unique way to thank Walter and June for their generosity.

Warren came up with the idea to write to the couple's classmates and tell them about the gift Walter and June had made. The letter suggested that the classmates contact Walter and June regarding their gift and express their personal appreciation. Taking into account the age of the couple (both were over 80), only a few classmates were still living. Most responded by sending notes.

Weeks later, Walter shared the letters that had come in from all across the country, extending appreciation to him and his wife for their benevolence. He never knew that the letters had been solicited; he just knew that their gift had been genuinely appreciated.

The Lesson

For those within an agency, the value of a gift, especially a large one, is obvious. Do not assume, however, that the importance of the gift has been conveyed to the donor. Those involved with the agency know what the money will accomplish, but a donor cannot understand its impact without having it interpreted.

One of the best ways to make the connection between the money and its value to others is to encourage others to reaffirm the importance of the gift. Board members, those influential in the community, and those important to the donor can convey their admiration in a meaningful way. Make sure this happens.

Go Beyond Recognition

The Principle

Many years ago during a Red Cross campaign, John, the head of the trust department of a major banking institution, stood up and addressed the campaign steering committee. This meeting was in preparation for an important fund-raising effort. As they discussed the campaign issues, John said it was his experience that recognition was not the issue for contributors. Instead, the issue was appreciation.

He was right. Donors want to know that their gifts make a difference. Because this is true, it is vital to give careful, premeditated consideration to the process of showing appreciation to donors.

Does this mean that public recognition is diminished? Certainly not. But appreciation—valuing the donor and recognizing the impact of the gift—is more important.

The Story

An older couple, Mary and Franklin, decided to give $3 million to build a wonderful, new facility for a senior services organization. This was substantially larger than any gift they had previously made. The couple enjoyed every moment of the process of breaking ground and constructing this new building. At the same time, their children were resentful that the agency had, in their minds, taken this money from the couple and ultimately from their inheritance.

Sensitive to their concern, an effort was made to take pictures and video of Mary and Franklin each time they visited the site. These photographs, which showed the couple wearing their hard hats and questioning the contractor, conveyed, as only pictures can, the couple's delight in being a part of this endeavor. Those pictures and written notes were sent to Mary and Franklin's children to share the energy, enthusiasm and love that this couple had for the project.

The children were also acknowledged for their importance to this project. This was done by asking them to join their parents in a family portrait. The portrait would be displayed in the finished building, recognizing that this was a gift, not just from the couple, but from the entire family. Mary and Franklin were especially delighted that this had been suggested.

The Lesson

While demonstrating true appreciation involves some cost, those costs are normally minimal. A small investment in appreciation can reap a large return; a donor who is genuinely appreciated will find it easier to continue to support a particular institution. On the other hand, the cost of not demonstrating appreciation can be huge. A donor who is not treated with appreciation will be less inclined to give in the future and will not refer others who might want to give.

These heartfelt gestures do not have to be expensive. The couple's photographs, for example, were a nominal expense, as were the stamps and letters. Adding the children to the portrait may have increased the cost of the portrait by a few hundred dollars, but the value to the family and to the project was priceless.

Look Outside the Fund-Raising Realm

The Principle

There is more fund-raising information in *Forbes* and *Fortune* than in virtually any typical fund-raising journal. While the amount of philanthropic information available has expanded significantly in the last several years, many books and magazines outside the fund-raising realm are tremendous resources of information.

The Story

Over the last several years, *The Millionaire Next Door* has been on the top ten best sellers list. Frequently, I ask large groups of fund raisers if they have read the book. Few have. They tell me that they do not need to learn how to be a millionaire. My answer is, "But you need to be prepared to know who they are." The book says little about philanthropy but volumes about how wealth is held in the country and by whom. Bea, Stanley, George, Jeanette, Milton, Mary, Frank and many others mentioned in this book are millionaires next door. Read that book. Then go find your million-dollar prospects.

Harvey Mackay's book *Dig the Well Before You Get Thirsty*, is the fund raiser's book on cultivation and preparation. On page after page, he describes the building of relationships. These are fund-raising skills.

He too has little to say about philanthropy and to the extent he does, I think he is wrong. The value is in the fund-raising professional learning how to use these tools.

Finally, we have all learned about the enormous transfer of wealth from one generation to the next. Do you think we learned this by reading fund-raising books and periodicals? No. This issue was first revealed in *Fortune* in the late 1980s.

The Lesson

Fund raisers must read a variety of periodicals in fields other than fund raising. Try these sources.

1.   Stanley, Thomas J. and Danko, William D., Ph.D. *The Millionaire Next Door.* Longstreet Press (1996).
2.   MacKay, Harvey. *Dig the Well Before You Get Thirsty.* Bantam Doubleday (1997).
3.   Beckwith, Harry. *Selling the Invisible: A Field Guide to Modern Marketing.* Warner Books, Inc. (1977).
4.   Gitomer, Jeffrey H. *Customer Satisfaction Is Worthless — Customer Loyalty Is Priceless.* Bard Press, (1998).
5.   Greene, Robert. *The 48 Laws of Power.* Penguin Books (1998).
6.   Collins, James. *Built to Last: Successful Habits of Visionary Companies.* Harper Business (1994).
7.   Scott, Steven K. *Simple Steps to Impossible Dreams.* Simon & Schuster (1998).
8.   Stanley, Thomas. *Selling to the Affluent.* McGraw-Hill (1997).
9.   Gitomer, Jeffrey H. *The Sales Bible.* William Morrow & Company (1994).
10. Silverman, Stephen M. *Where There's a Will.* Harper Collins Publishers (1991).

Subscribe to the *Wall Street Journal* and other business publications, and read them. Do not look at philanthropy as a one-event sport. It is a decathlon of financial acumen—business, management, economics, taxes, estate planning, Social Security. Take advantage of the wealth of information available.

Ask For the Gift of Affiliation

The Principle

Donors not only make financial commitments to institutions, they also invest their reputations, their integrity and their knowledge. For a wide variety of reasons, many donors wish to remain anonymous. In fact, it takes great courage to be publicly named as a donor of a large gift. Some families have been threatened, and at the very least, such recognition encourages additional solicitations. Still, the public acknowledgment of association is tremendously helpful to any agency, especially one that is not known for receiving large donations.

The Story

Mary Margaret had never given to the community health center, an organization that offered medical care for undeserved people in her city. Allen, the executive director, who also doubled as the fund raiser, needed extra space to develop the facility. He discovered that the land north of the agency's property was owned in trust by Mary Margaret. Allen had never spoken to Mary Margaret, and he did not know who she was or how she was associated with the land. He had no idea what the land had been used for in past, only that it now stood empty, and he needed it.

After further investigation, Allen located a friend of Mary Margaret's, Tim, an affluent physician who regularly supported the community health center. Because of Tim's friendship with both Allen and Mary Margaret, he was asked to arrange a meeting. The doctor reluctantly agreed. Mary Margaret had become a rather private person following the death of her husband, yet Dr. Tim felt that this might be something that would bring her rich satisfaction.

Allen was interested in one quarter of the block directly north of the health center. Mary Margaret felt that only Allen's group would ever be interested in this particular piece of property. Some advisors suggested that she hold out for a good price, but since the property was not being rented and she was simply paying taxes, she agreed to make the gift.

Allen asked Mary Margaret to donate the land and invited her to be profiled in their fund-raising efforts to build the additional facility. He let her know that her gift, which was valued at more than $250,000, was magnificent and greatly appreciated, and yet there was something else she could give that would be of equal value. If the community knew how strongly Mary Margaret felt about this project, that awareness would have a great impact on others. Giving the land had cost her some money, but the tougher decision was whether or not to establish a public affiliation. After some consideration, she agreed.

This association continued to develop. Mary Margaret became a volunteer at the center and eventually considered Allen a very close friend. She joined the board of directors, and as one of the very few non-client members of the board, she spoke out strongly on behalf of the center. Not surprisingly, she received other requests, which she declined. She already had a wonderful avenue for philanthropy.

The Lesson

The gift of affiliation is valuable. When a donor lends her standing in the community to a project, it should be honored and appreciated.

Stay Ahead Of the Competition

Campaign 2000

"No winner can hope to stay ahead of the competition by standing still," said Emporia State University President, Robert E. Glennen in February 1994 while announcing the beginning of Campaign 2000. The University was seeking more than $25 million in a five-year period to fund five specific areas of education. In less than four years the University exceeded its goal with gifts of more than $26 million in capital and endowment dollars.

Emporia State University (ESU) was founded in 1863 as the Kansas State Normal School to prepare teachers. ESU, one of six institutions in the Kansas Board of Regents system, has an enrollment of more than 5000 students. The success of Campaign 2000 assured the continuation of the University's national and international profiles in Education and Library and Information Management and stimulated other programs to develop their own reputations for excellence.

Campaign 2000 represented an opportunity to secure necessary financial resources for student quality and diversity, teaching excellence, educational foundations for the future, serving the citizens of kansas, and physical plant.

Student Quality and Diversity

To continue to meet the needs of its students, the University was seeking scholarships to recruit and retain academically, artistically and athletically talented students. Funding was needed to enhance specific academic programs, grants to give special students the chance at a higher education, and assistance to expand education beyond the normal classroom setting.

Teaching Excellence

Attracting and retaining an outstanding faculty and staff is essential. Not only does the most fundamental mission provide classroom instruction of the highest possible caliber, but it also helps enhance the University's reputation among its peers and the general public.

Educational Foundations for the Future

The entire campus needed to be connected through fiber optics and then linked to offer networks—school districts in Kansas and throughout the nation, other Kansas Board of Regents institutions, and vital database networks around the world. This goal was met with a state-of-the-art computer lab installed in the English department.

Dr. Russ Meyers, a professor in the English department at ESU, commented, "I have spent eight years at two different universities trying to get such a computer lab/classroom. I thought it would take four to five years, but we got it within one year. What I have been struggling to do for eight years, we did in one year at Emporia State University. We now have state-of-the-art equipment and software for our journalism students."

Serving the Citizens of Kansas

A key component of Emporia State University's mission is to serve the needs of Kansas citizens in specific areas outside the classroom. Since its inception, ESU has sought and fostered partnerships with schools and businesses to recognize individual excellence, protect and promote innovative programs unique to this region, and establish centers for excellence in areas that support the University's mission.

Physical Plant

Some programs at ESU had outgrown their facilities and many existing facilities needed maintenance, repair, renovation and upgrading. The quality of facilities—whether in the classroom, laboratory, library or rehearsal hall—and the learning environment affected the quality of instruction.

Trustees also wanted to provide an opportunity to add dimension to ESU's reputation and public perception, in terms of both geographic orientation and academic focus. Campaign 2000 let more people in on the well-kept secret that ESU is a diverse and contemporary institution of higher learning with much to offer students and faculty who prefer the benefits of an intimate learning environment. Although the total needs of the University far exceeded the items selected for funding, the Trustees were uncomfortable setting a $25 million goal because of the psychological hurdle. Past impressions still shadowed ESU's vision for the future.

Robert Swanson who served two years as the director of development and one year as CEO of the Emporia State University Foundation explained: "We found the local community supported the campaign, but many people shared a skepticism similar to that held by the Trustees. ESU was established as the *teachers college* for Kansas in 1863. We produce great teachers, but they obviously do not generate the same wealth during their lifetimes as doctors and lawyers," Swanson said.

A surprising fact to Swanson and the Trustees was that ESU alumni were more than willing to help their alma mater when the case was presented to them. The total number of donors tripled during the first three years of the campaign. "Gifts from five teachers exceeded $200,000," Swanson said.

Campaign 2000 also changed the management and organization of the Emporia State University Foundation. The positive growing pains and re-structuring that resulted from Campaign

2000's success increased employees at the Foundation from four to 10.

Kimera Maxwell served as the Foundation's CEO for much of the campaign. "With our consultant's guidance, Campaign 2000 forged valuable relationships between the institution and its donors and we realized how good stewardship of these relationships can play a critical role in future planning."

Emporia State University overcame temptations of self-doubt and instead, took bold steps to secure a vision of growth and a reputation of excellence.

Campaign 2000 not only added finances, it laid a foundation for future success.

Demonstrating the Gift's Impact— Making a Difference

ABCs Of Affiliation

The Principle

Rather than allowing a donor to "window shop" at the institution, take her in and involve her. If the donor gives to a children's home, invite the donor to have dinner there with the children. If she makes a gift to acquire an art collection, involve her in an advisory role with the next exhibition. If a donor gives to a scholarship fund, make sure she has a chance to get to know the scholarship recipients.

Provide ways for donors to experience the ABCs of affiliation:

- Appreciation *for* the agency
- Belief *in* the agency
- Commitment *to* the agency

Each progression further involves the donors, and they feel that they are part of the institution. Donors can "appreciate" an agency from a distance, but "believing" means they understand and approve of the agency's work. "Commitment" establishes a personal association and affirmation of the agency's efforts. Through involvement, donors are no longer on the outside looking in; they are a vital part of the work being accomplished.

The Story

Newton was proud of the $5 million endowment that he had made to the local university. In fact, Newton and his wife, Rosie, understood the importance of a quality education through their own life experiences and the lives of their children. While Newton was a successful businessman, he believed his success was due to luck. He always yearned for a college education. Their endowment gift allowed them to pay back some of that "luck."

It was not until after Newton had given the gift and his scholarship recipients began to grow in numbers that he figured out a way to measure this scholarship project. Their fund provided scholarships for about 50 students per year. Of course, after the first few years as the corpus grew, the fund was adding about 10 students a year as 10 students would graduate. Newton developed a formula based on the extra income a college graduate on the average made over that of a non-college graduate. He then took his number of graduates times this amount and added a 40-year inflation factor—40 years was roughly the income-producing time after college for his graduates. Newton calculated the millions and ultimately billions of dollars his scholarship fund would generate for the economy which would benefit the whole of society.

Impact can be measured in a number of ways. Newton, always a numbers guy, found his impact in numbers.

The Lesson

Help donors value the impact of their gifts. If this is accomplished, the greater the chances are for a future gift. A tangible way to deepen commitment is to involve donors in the impact of their gifts through personal experience.

You Only Make a First Impression Once

The Principle

An agency may do tremendous work and be worthy of support, but if a fund raiser reflects something less impressive, the institution loses out. This is sad but true, and entirely avoidable.

Being disheveled or dressing inappropriately sends a message of lack of respect. A friend and colleague, Murray Blackwelder, used to say, "You can always take off your tie, but you can't put one on if you don't have it." When in doubt, dress well.

Words need to be chosen as carefully as clothing. "It is just a matter of semantics" is never an excuse for poorly chosen words. In philanthropy, words are always consequential. In demeanor, both insecurity and arrogance damage developing relationships. Humility and confidence are not incompatible.

The fund raiser also needs to have appropriate telephone skills. Often communication with a prospect is not in person. It is important not to talk too softly, too loudly, or too quickly.

The Story

Several years ago, Steve worked as a philanthropic consultant to Karl Menninger for The Villages, a part of Menninger's program. In one telephone conversation with Menninger, his wife, Jean, joined the conversation on an extension. Steve indicated that something needed to occur in August. Almost 100 years old at that time, Menninger shouted to his wife, "Steve wants us to have an audit!" Alarmed, Steve said, "No, we need to do this in *August*." While the misunderstanding may sound a little humorous today, it illustrates an important point. Fund raisers must know how they are being heard.

Another example comes from a university president, Roger, who had a very soft, soothing voice. This was quite reassuring in person, but over the phone it could be counterproductive. When it came to phone solicitations, his gentle voice masked a sense of conviction and zeal for his message. In one setting Roger's voice was an asset, but in a different situation it was an impediment. Awareness of this allows for correction and adaptation where necessary.

The Lesson

Be conscious of appearance, attitude and verbal expression. Organize your thoughts before you make the call. Be sensitive to the particular needs of your donor. These add up to a positive first impression.

Gifts that Come To Life

The Principle

Conventional wisdom says that it is easier to raise money for the construction or renovation of a building than it is to raise money for an endowment. Endowments are less familiar. Historically, endowments were only established by the very wealthy and financially sophisticated. However, this view of endowments is no longer valid.

Endowments may appear less tangible than buildings and may seem to have less name recognition, but appearances can be misleading. In fact, the perpetual nature of an endowment can make it the most appealing of giving options. Endowments represent a wonderful opportunity to attach a sense of permanence to philanthropy.

The Story

Nathan and Mary desired widespread and significant recognition for their family name. That desire resulted from the loss of several members of their family both young and old. The couple had been personally devastated in ways that no family should. At first, they were interested in naming a building in honor of loved ones. They could easily envision a child care facility—with rooms, equipment, and playgrounds.

Subsequently, they became aware of the possibility of establishing an endowment. An endowment, however, was more difficult to imagine.

After many conversations with the agency's development officers and careful consideration, Nathan and Mary realized that an endowment could well be a longer-lasting memorial than a building. When the couple chose to donate several million dollars through an endowment, they told the development director, "Larry, this gift will go on forever." Larry acknowledged that the endowment would help others for many years to come, long after many buildings have deteriorated.

The Lesson

Endowments allow donors to give in perpetuity. This can be an enormous comfort and appeal.

Investment Management Breeds Confidence

The Principle

Virtually all donors know the value of a dollar and do not view waste with indifference. Furthermore, donors realize that waste is not simply spending more than necessary. Waste also occurs when money is allowed to remain virtually inactive in a savings account, bearing an unnecessarily low interest rate. On the other hand, jeopardizing money through risky financial vehicles is unwise. Good money management exists somewhere between the two extremes.

It is valuable for a fund raiser to demonstrate to donors that their investments are receiving a high level of return. Cornell University's recent literature concerning its endowment highlighted this area of financial management. The return on money invested had grown at an annual average of ten percent for an extended number of years. Cornell also included an extensive profile of its investment committee—names, backgrounds, performance levels and experience. These give donors confidence that they are advancing a successful endowment.

The Story

Frank gave more than $10 million to a performing arts center foundation several years ago. He was later asked to join the board of trustees and upon joining, discovered that the board's investment strategy was yielding the equivalent of a passbook savings account. Frank expected the board to manage the center's extensive resources more profitably. Since his gift now represented almost one-third of the foundation's assets, Frank demanded a much more aggressive investment strategy. As a result of Frank's leadership and the new investment strategy, the assets doubled in a short time.

The Lesson

Donors are accustomed to reviewing the prospectus of a mutual fund before investing. They know how to glance down to the "P/E" column of profit and earnings data. Agencies that want to continue to perform must do so in an environment that includes good investment research and demonstrates solid stewardship.

A Timeline
Is a
Plan

The Principle

A timeline is essential to the preparation and progress of any organization's fund-raising efforts. More than a calendar of events, a well-planned timeline is an indispensable map that outlines the path of predetermined goals that add up to success. A timeline reflects all the important milestones established by an agency in order to help maintain, for staff and volunteers, a common vision and coordinated implementation.

The timeline indicates the function of various donors, volunteers and staff positions and shows when certain tasks should be performed. Donor identification, cultivation, qualification, and solicitation are mapped out in sequence. The timeline lists the modes of communication to be utilized—written and oral, private and public. A complete timeline even delineates policies that must be developed and indicates when this will be accomplished.

The Lesson

A timeline reveals *what* still needs to be done and *when*. Because staff members and volunteers are able to see the sequence of tasks, they can be unified in their efforts and more realistic in their expectations.

The following is an example of a 2 year campaign timeline. The importance is the illustration of time parameters.

Campaign Time Line

	First Year								
	JAN	FEB	MAR	APR	MAY	JUN	JUL	AUG	SEP
Re-Draft of Case Statement	■								
Goal Setting	■								
Leadership Selection									
Steering Committee Selection									
Steering Committee Meeting									
$25,000 + prospects									
Identification									
Cultivation									
Solicitation									
$10,000 + prospects									
Identification									
Cultivation									
Solicitation									
$1,000 + prospects									
Identification									
Cultivation									
Solicitation									
General Solicitation (under $1,000)									
Volunteer Training			■						
Recognition Policy Approval									
Appreciation Policy Approval									
Gift Acceptance Policy Approval									
Stewardship Policy Approval									
Publications			■			■			

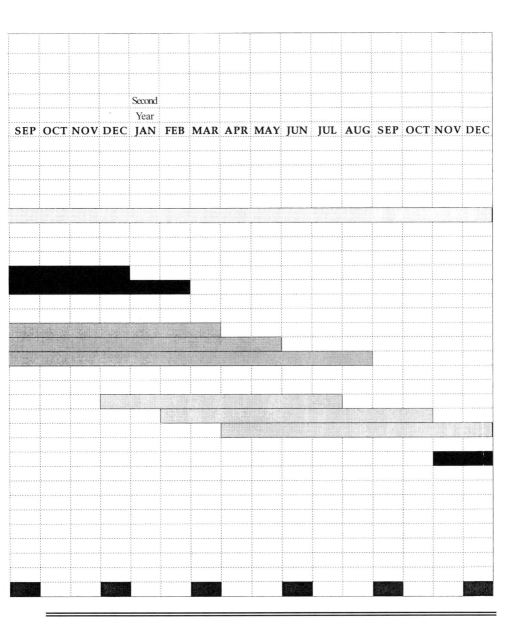

Perpetuate The Donor's Passion

The Principle

Donors frequently make gifts to spotlight values they consider important.

The Story

Jack had attended the same church for several decades and admired his pastor, Dr. Jim. Throughout the years, Dr. Jim had exemplified, through his character and focus, values that Jack shared wholeheartedly.

Jack believed that when Dr. Jim retired, the pastor's name and reputation needed to be remembered. Jack approached the seminary from which Dr. Jim had graduated and suggested establishing a chair named in Dr. Jim's honor. The president of the seminary was initially reluctant to immediately create the proposed chair, due to his concern about Jack's three-year payment schedule. The seminary president was concerned that Jack would not complete his gift pledge and the seminary would have hired someone they could not support. A modified funding plan, allowing Jack to provide the funding for the endowment as well as annually funding the chair until the endowment was totally in place, alleviated these concerns, and a qualified professor was named to that chair.

Jack was able to publicly honor Dr. Jim and provide an avenue for their shared values to be perpetuated. Jack's gift placed Dr. Jim's life in plain view, encouraging others that solid values and a life of integrity were worthy of emulation.

Incidentally, in keeping with the values he shared with Dr. Jim, Jack donated his gift anonymously.

The Lesson

Listen carefully to the donor's passion. Look for ways to connect with the donor's core values or someone who epitomizes those beliefs. How can the donor's zeal and appreciation for another individual translate into a tangible expression? Great devotion is a strong motivation to give.

Promote Integrity

The Principle

In the absence of a tangible product, an organization that provides charitable services finds that its standing in the community is its greatest asset. When an individual, corporation or foundation decides to invest in an organization through a gift, the perceived integrity of the organization rises dramatically.

The Story

Bill represented a major national foundation. He reviewed one appeal for funds from a small, nonprofit social service agency that needed funds for a new facility and to implement a program to manage the facility. Bill's foundation investigated the agency and discovered that it had a history of being unable to meet its payroll obligations, as well as other problems.

Bill confronted the agency's leaders and encouraged them to develop a plan for rebuilding the agency's reputation in the community. Although not catastrophic, these problems deserved the agency's attention. Rather than responding defensively, the agency's leaders appreciated Bill's comments. After honestly evaluating the situation, the agency's leaders developed a plan to improve its operation.

As a result of the social work agency's commitment to improvement, Bill's foundation earmarked $1 million toward its funding. The foundation assisted in the development of the agency's new facility and provided the transition money necessary to implement its operational plan.

The Lesson

Do not respond defensively to criticisms by other organizations or by individuals within the agency. View these comments as instructive and constructive criticisms that can enhance the ability of the agency to perform in the future.

You Are the Institution

The Principle

For many donors, particularly those who live great distances from an institution, the periodic presence of the fund-raising representative reflects directly upon that institution. Over time, this connection (supported by routine newsletters and other means of communication) becomes the basis of the relationship between the donor and the institution.

What may first appear to be simple administrative decisions—such as who to meet for breakfast, see at lunch, or invite to dinner—can make or break relationships. The choices concerning invitations to receptions or ceremonies become important when seen through the eyes of those who are not invited. No fund raiser ever handles these situations flawlessly. Well-planned contacts with consistent follow-through make the difference in the long run.

The Story

Michael was a fund-raising representative for a small college with a national constituency. Each time he visited a large city, Michael was careful to meet the prominent people associated with the institution he represented. He repeatedly reviewed the alumni list, making those important decisions about which people to meet for breakfast, lunch and dinner. Frequently, he located foundations that needed follow-up. He also stopped by the local newspaper often to make sure the society editor covered the institution's gatherings and reported them accurately. Periodically, Michael held alumni events.

For all his efforts around town, Michael continually neglected Jean, a woman in her 90s, who had attended the university decades earlier. Jean had made a commitment through her estate that could eventually be worth more than $7 million to the university. Still, Jean was never on the breakfast list, the dinner list, the luncheon list or the reception list. She received occasional invitations to alumni events, but she was never given the personal follow-up deserving of a major donor. When asked how she felt about this neglect, Jean said, "Well, I know they are very busy, and they have a lot of important people to see. But I would like to hear from them once in a while to know what they need."

Jean was not a difficult prospect to uncover. She was a widow, and her only child died. She lived in an upscale retirement community in a city that Michael visited; nevertheless, he did not know her. She had no community profile and was never sought out, nor was a relationship ever cultivated.

Jean will likely leave the university's provision in her estate plans because she is a woman true to her word. Yet, in the current atmosphere of expediency and self-interest, there will certainly be fewer and fewer people like Jean.

The Lesson

Fund raisers must never take donors for granted.

To Find Quality Staff, Go to the Source

The Principle

Harvard does not produce high caliber graduates solely on the basis of their educational program. Instead, they start with high caliber students. Quality begets quality. This is also true for fund-raising and philanthropic institutions.

While there are limitations to finances designated for various salaries, when selecting someone to represent the institution as a fund raiser, the person of highest quality and character should get the job, not the person who will work for the smallest salary. After hiring an individual, give that person the tools and opportunities to become successful.

The Story

David was associated with a large gift from a high profile donor at one social service agency. Subsequently he was hired by a different institution at a salary significantly greater than he was probably worth as a fund raiser. While David was one of several fund raisers who worked on this major gift, he was not the primary force behind it. The new agency wanted to raise larger gifts and believed that the support of a fund raiser from a larger organization would guarantee such gifts. After failing to complete the fund-raising assignment, he moved on to yet another agency. The previous employers then wonder what happened.

The problem was that this person's ability to raise money was overestimated. In fund raising, it is very easy to look successful. By being associated with large gifts, it is common for an individual to build a set of credentials that are somewhat misleading. Agencies hungry for success are willing to overlook problems.

The Lesson

The quality of philanthropy is best articulated by donors who have been solicited. Agencies hiring fund raisers should always ask the candidates to identify two or three donors who will allow themselves to be interviewed. For an accurate assessment, it is best to go to the source.

Put the Donor's Objectives First

The Principle

Always put the donor first. Find natural ways to get to know donors and show respect for what they have accomplished. For example, ask open-ended questions such as, "How did you get involved in this business?" Then listen. Not passive, obligatory listening but active, deliberate listening. Not talking is not the same thing as listening. True listening involves empathy and understanding. Take hold of what is said to identify the donor's needs and desires so you can give them true consideration. Try to determine how these objectives can best be related to the institution.

The Story

A donor's needs can be personal, professional, cultural, environmental, financial, etc. Justin's were personal. He was interested in securing a facility for his wife who was afflicted with Alzheimer's disease. Since there were no facilities in his area that met his expectations, he envisioned a new state-of-the-art facility for the care of people with Alzheimer's. When Justin shared his vision for the project, everyone understood his commitment to the projects success. People deeply respected Justin, not only because of his sincerity, but also because they realized their own frailty in the light of this indiscriminate disease.

The Lesson

While an agency has a need to generate contributions, donors often have an equally genuine need to give. The ability to impact the lives of people in need gives a donor hope, joy, and a renewed quality of life. By listening and caring about the donor's deepest needs, a fund raiser can help the donor reach his objectives.

Listen to the donor. Think about the donor's needs carefully. Put the donor's needs at the forefront of your fund-raising efforts.

Few People Give to Sand Sculptures

The Principle

Donors want to know that the agencies and institutions they support are secure. The "squeaky wheel" fund-raising tactics of the 1980s proved to be short-lived. Although donors came to the rescue repeatedly, the emergencies became predictable and about as believable as a "Going Out of Business" sign. A fund raiser who believes that solicitation is best accomplished by continually presenting the newest "crisis" may end up creating his own personal crisis—job hunting.

The Story

Neil served as the volunteer chairman of an important new institution whose purpose was to build a museum honoring the fields of science and technology. Neil solicited the largest gift to the campaign and continued to provide fund-raising and solicitation leadership.

More pivotal than Neil's work with solicitation was the stewardship he provided. He constantly reviewed and analyzed cash-flow projections, business plans and programs. Neil also accurately determined the capital cost estimate for the project. His gift to this institution was the ability to create an atmosphere of stability that gave this project permanency.

The Lesson

Few people want to invest in a sand sculpture. Donors are attracted to projects with staying power. An agency that demonstrates stability and thoroughness in its plans and goals is viewed as a sound investment. Share with donors the effectiveness and good business sense demonstrated by the agency.

Greet Them With Your Best

The Principle

Most often agencies consider the job of receptionist an entry-level position. In reality, this job requires as much expertise as many other administrative positions within an institution. A receptionist must handle the challenge of juggling calls while greeting visitors, receiving and disseminating accurate messages and serving as a clearing house for other administrative needs. This must be done with the grace and effortlessness of a polished host or hostess—no easy task by any stretch of the imagination.

This role should be filled by a highly skilled and well-trained employee because over the phone and in person, the receptionist often makes the first impression for an institution. Too often, institutions overlook the vital role of their receptionists.

The Story

A major national corporation in Kansas City employed a receptionist who had been with the company for at least a decade. This receptionist remembered the names of visitors, their associations, and with whom they usually met, even if they visited only once a year. She was able to make visitors feel welcome at the headquarters. A sort of living, breathing greeting card, she embodied the values of the institution.

In contrast, a few years ago another company in the same city decided to automate its reception area. Instead of signing in with a receptionist, visitors logged on to a computer, giving their names and other information. Although this company wanted to showcase its advanced technology, many visitors were not impressed. One older gentleman shared his consternation at having to stand blankly in front of a strange screen, too intimidated to attempt to operate this unfamiliar piece of machinery and too embarrassed to ask for help. Instead, he opted to leave. Whatever the motivation, this company chose hardware over humanity—not a good way to encourage lasting relationships.

In one fund-raising office, the director of client relations consistently received incredibly positive comments for how she treated people in person and on the phone. Additionally, positive comments regarding her knowledge and skills were common. When she had her first child, several clients sent cards and gifts, even though they had never met her. She had the ability to make people feel important and valued.

The Lesson

Put the best people at the front door. Do not underestimate the power of this position. Treat these individuals as important members of the team, and the institution will benefit.

Benefiting the Community First

Boys & Girls Clubs and Genesis School

A $424,000 land gift served as the catalyst for a successful three-year fund-raising project that has generated nearly $9 million for the renovation and expansion of the John T. Thornberry Boys & Girls Clubs.

A collaborative effort of the Boys & Girls Clubs and Genesis School, an alternative middle school, the campaign has exceeded its original $8.5 million goal and generated $8,966,550.

The result will be the Thornberry Center for Youth and Families (TCYF), a center providing an array of services to develop and nurture adolescents and strengthen families.

"We're hoping to complete the renovation by early spring of the year 2000," David A. Smith, president of the Boys & Girls Club said. "This is an outstanding example of two non-profit organizations collaborating on a project that will benefit not only themselves, but the community."

The Plan of Action

In response to the overwhelming need for youth development and family-focused services throughout the urban core, the volunteer leadership of the two agencies set out in June, 1995, to create the Thornberry Center for Youth and Families.

The project was a landlord/tenant model of collaboration, with the Boys & Girls Clubs as the owner and Genesis School as the tenant with equity interest. Both agencies agreed to a limited public campaign because of a desire not to impact annual fund support.

The project expanded the facility by more than 40,000 square feet. About 22,000 square feet will be available for public and private organizations, neighborhood and youth groups. A second gymnasium will draw more youth to overall services at the facility, which includes a broad range of youth development activities.

The First Steps

It took one and a half years of planning to establish the campaign that would result in the successful generation of capital for the project.

"When the land was made available, I approached the Genesis School director about a collaborative effort," Smith said. "The school was leasing 6,500 square feet from us and also needed to expand, so they were extremely excited about the project."

The Genesis School had previously retained Hartsook and Associates, a Wichita-based consulting firm, to complete a feasibility study for a Genesis School capital campaign. The consultant was subsequently employed to revise the study, by adding The Boys & Girls Clubs and providing consulting services for the collaborative effort of the two agencies.

Smith said fund-raising efforts were enhanced not only by the community's current philanthropy boom but also by the agencies' long-standing reputations in the community.

Originally started as the Boys Hotel, the Boys & Girls Clubs have been in existence since 1912. This provided a safe alternative to the streets and a positive place for children and adolescents, ages seven to 17. The center serves approximately 4,500 children annually.

Genesis School originated in 1975 as a VISTA project. It is a community-based middle school that incorporates alternative strategies for students who have experienced difficulties in traditional school settings.

"Between us, we have been serving the community about 100 years," Smith said. "We have a lot of credibility, as well as boards of directors comprised of well-known community leaders who are instrumental in the fund-raising efforts."

The expansion increased the capacity of both agencies, allowing Genesis School to increase its enrollment by 50 percent and provide adequate space for students to pursue the arts, media and other forms of social expression. The Boys & Girls Clubs increased the number of youth served at the site to an estimated 1,000 youth per day during the summer and 650 daily during the school year.

The Campaign

The campaign took off when the consulting firm helped the agencies establish the Capital Campaign Leadership Committee which included about 20 key players in the community.

Well-known community leaders Gordon and Nancy Beaham and Barnett and Shirley Helzberg served as honorary chairs. Albert P. Mauro, a respected capital campaign veteran in the area, served as general chairman.

The consultant worked with a steering committee to establish campaign goals, expense projections, a prospect/donor list and a timeline. The list included more than 70 potential donors.

"The consultant helped with prospect identification and screening efforts," Smith said. "And once we had established our goal to raise

$8.5 million, he set about to create a system and structure to accomplish it using committees, materials and leads."

In addition to being intimate with the campaign and providing strategies during its inevitable ups and downs, the consultant provided both motivation for campaign workers and credibility for potential donors, Smith said.

"We wouldn't have been as successful without the consultant's advice and leadership," Smith said. "Potential donors expect you to have a consultant who will steer you in the right direction. They knew we were up to snuff and they felt better about their investment."

The Results

In addition to two gifts of more than $500,000, the campaign received two challenge grants: a $500,000 matching grant from the Kresge Foundation and a promise of $1.8 million from the Mabee Foundation, if the agencies could raise the total goal.

Other major donors included NationsBank Private Client Group, $400,000; Sprint, $250,000; and the Kauffman Foundation, $500,000. Other contributions ranged from $500 to $200,000.

The campaign advanced more rapidly than the original timeline and reached and exceeded the original $8.5 million goal ahead of schedule.

Fund Raiser, Let's Get Personal

Ban
The Big
Brag

The Principle

When a fund raiser succeeds at raising substantial sums, he can be tempted to brag. However, a realistic sense of humility is the most appropriate outlook, especially after a successful solicitation.

Bragging about gifts demeans both the fund raiser and the donor and may cause the donor to decide to choose a different target for future philanthropy.

The Story

A major capital funds drive was established to build a new nursing facility in a retirement community. Jim, the director of development, succeeded in securing a $1 million gift from Sarah. That commitment enabled the project to advance and boosted the confidence of the volunteer leadership.

While Jim was unquestionably a critical component in securing the gift, he wanted everyone to know that he had, single-handedly made the gift happen.

In his conversations with volunteers and others, he shared the intimate details of how the donor relationship had been cultivated. He described the unfolding drama of what led up to the actual solicitation, as well as the specific language and emotion of the important moment of asking for the gift. In detail, he revealed Sarah's responses as she had contemplated making her commitment to the center.

Unfortunately, Sarah became aware of the indiscreet manner in which Jim was discussing these private details. Sarah responded gently and discreetly. She invited Jim to lunch. He arrived promptly, anticipating the opportunity to solicit another large gift. Sarah told Jim what she had heard in the retirement community and asked Jim if it was true. Had he, in fact, boasted about the solicitation process?

Jim was stunned. To his credit, he admitted his mistake and sought her forgiveness.

Sarah explained that the gift was neither for *him*, nor about *him*. The motivation behind the gift was the deep desire on her part to preserve the *dignity* of those suffering and to support and encourage the families of the residents. Sarah indicated that if she ever heard of his boasting about her gift again, she would see that he was never given responsibility or credit for any future gift she might make.

Jim painfully learned the value of humility and discretion in fund raising.

The Lesson

The process of soliciting and receiving of philanthropy is an intimate, quiet event. Mutual success of the donor, agency, and fund raiser can be celebrated and shared in many ways. However, the fund raiser must respect the privacy of the donor. In appropriate circumstances, the fund raiser should emphasize the donor's achievement in giving. Reveling in the act of the giver, rather than the achievement of the fund raiser, is the only appropriate response from the fund raiser.

Remember: While some fund raisers are talking about their latest gifts, others are quietly soliciting even larger ones.

Let's Talk Money

The Principle

Discussing finances puts a fund raiser in an uncomfortable position. Recent research regarding this topic indicates that many fund raisers are uncomfortable with affluent individuals; others may actually be openly hostile to people with wealth. This uneasiness is incongruous with the fund raiser's need to talk comfortably about large sums of money. To offset this tendency, a fund raiser should introduce issues dealing with money early in the relationship.

In order to be comfortable discussing money issues, the fund raiser needs to be knowledgeable about business, commerce and finance. A fund raiser can increase fiscal knowledge by reading *Fortune, Forbes, Business Week* and other financial publications. Current information is available virtually around the clock on cable business channels and on the radio. One can easily stay current on the major issues.

Additionally, the fund raiser should be generally aware of those important financial transactions occurring in the donor prospect's local community.

One of the best ways to gain familiarity with financial concerns is to ask questions and seek advice from prospects. It is important to learn as much as possible about how money is generated, accumulated and protected.

The Story

Francis was intrigued by the idea of making a multimillion-dollar gift to a certain hospital but was reluctant to actually commit. Mark, the fund raiser, bantered with Francis that he thought Francis had a $10 million gift in him, just waiting to be given. Mark kept up with Francis regarding this gift opportunity, joking with him over a period of months. A natural relationship developed and, in a relaxed but confident manner, Mark continued to cultivate this prospect genuinely and patiently.

Throughout this relationship, Francis jokingly reminded Mark just how much money that was and how hard it was to earn that much money in the first place. Under the circumstances, Francis could not see himself giving a gift of that magnitude.

As a major stockholder in a large company, Francis was frequently listed in the newspaper, along with the number of shares he held in the company. This type of information—who sits on what boards, who owns what publicly-held companies—is available to anyone, due to laws dealing with public records.

One Friday, the stock market took a sudden and severe downward correction. Because Francis' holdings were well-known, it was easy to calculate that in one day he had lost, at least on paper, more than $10 million. At a Saturday brunch, Mark, who had been keeping abreast of financial news, met Francis and commented, "I saw what happened in the market yesterday. I guess I lost my gift in that downturn." Francis looked up from his brunch, smiled, and responded, "It's only on paper. It comes and it goes."

In that brief exchange was the recognition that the donor had finally settled the issue mentally. It was clear that his gift was going to be of the size that Mark had been suggesting throughout their light-hearted joking. Not long after that, the exact amount was confirmed, and the gift was closed within ten days of that meeting.

Mark's awareness of Francis' financial considerations and of events in the market provided the impetus for that kind of jovial rapport surrounding the discussion of money.

The Lesson

Fund raising is financial by nature. It is important to stay in touch with the general state of the economy, reasonably familiar with various financial aspects, and continually inquisitive about the activities of money in general.

Loose
Lips
Sink
Ships

The Principle

Fund raising is a competitive enterprise, whether we like it or not, whether we admit it or not. While it is good for a fund raiser to be mentally and emotionally committed to an agency, he should never, for any reason, criticize another agency. First, the information might be wrong. Second, even if it is right, the tactic of criticizing is wrong. Finally, justified or not, criticism may have a different effect than intended on a prospect.

The Story

Nancy was a dedicated development officer, committed to the children's center for which she worked. She valued and appreciated the institution, which she felt could do no wrong. When soliciting Paul and Sylvia for a donation, she contrasted her agency to another one in the area with a similar mission. She recounted to the couple stories that she had heard about the agency and gave her interpretation of those problems. Nancy highlighted some of the personnel issues confronted by the other agency and generally left the impression that the competition was a poor excuse for an alternative to her own group.

Nancy had researched the donor, but overlooked one piece of information. Sylvia's half-brother, who did not share her maiden name, was the chief financial officer of the other agency. After listening to the litany of criticisms, Paul asked Nancy how she had gained so much insight into the competition. He queried her as to how her agency remained immune to such challenges—challenges common to most institutions. No answer would have been sufficient.

Paul concluded by advising Nancy that in the future she had better get her facts straight. No gift was offered to Nancy's agency. Instead, Paul and Sylvia gave $1.5 million to the other institution.

The Lesson

Never talk negatively about other institutions. A fund raiser's attitude should be all construction and zero demolition. All energy and focus should be poured into building up one's own institution, not tearing down another.

Timing Is Everything

The Principle

Being punctual will never get you into trouble. It is not necessary to become an automaton, inflexible and incapable of spontaneity, but it is vital that a fund raiser be punctual. Be on time, all of the time. When that is just not possible, make sure to let people know about the delay. Unexplained tardiness is inexcusable.

The Story

While conducting a study for a hospital with a national reputation, Jim, a fund raiser, traveled to New York to visit with Harold, a major prospect. Harold had recently become a billionaire and had many reasons to care about the institution Jim represented. Jim arrived in New York and drove a hundred miles outside of New York City to arrive at Harold's office on time. Harold was late, and Jim was given a tour of the building. Staff members supplied refreshments and invited Jim to make phone calls, which he did.

Almost two hours later, Harold arrived and very apologetically and thoroughly described the reason for his tardiness. Jim accepted Harold's explanation, and the meeting went well. Harold ultimately gave $10 million. Harold later told Jim's employer that he valued Jim's willingness to accept his apology. Harold felt that if Jim's behavior represented how the hospital treated people, he had made the correct decision to give.

The Lesson

Be the one who is on time. Allow for delays in traffic. Plan for last-minute phone calls. Get there early, if possible, to reflect and prepare before walking into the meeting.

Lighten Up

The Principle

People take fund raising seriously, and indeed, they should. Raising funds for important causes certainly is a mission of high calling. However, some fund raisers take themselves far too seriously.

The Story

Charles and Felecia were small contributors to a local community food bank. They enjoyed the annual events such as food baskets, Thanksgiving food donations, and holiday food distribution. It became very important to them. Charles served on the board and Felecia, who had served on the board in the past, continued to work as a volunteer. The food bank grew until the need for additional land and facilities became obvious. Even without extravagant plans, the total cost of the expansion was estimated at $1 million.

When Charles and Felecia were asked about the food bank's ability to raise $1 million, they were not very optimistic. The agency's board had plenty of representation statewide and locally, but the board members had very little wealth. Gina, the executive director, made an appointment to talk with the couple about the campaign. She had a terrific sense of humor and was able to find joy even in the most difficult circumstances. Gina helped people see the humor in life and recognize difficulty as opportunity. Although her job was serious, she always had a good story and a great smile.

During her meeting with Charles and Felecia, Gina had a chance to outline the needs of the food bank. Due to his work on the board, Charles had valuable insight. Felecia, too, because of her volunteer work, was able to make useful suggestions. Gina looked at both of them and asked, "Do you really think we can raise $1 million?"

Charles said, "I know the board does not have much money."

Felecia added, "I do not think the volunteers are really able to help much financially, either."

Gina, agreeing with their assessment, added her observation, "I guess you two are the only ones who really have any money to give."

Intrigued by the comment, Felecia asked, "So then, Gina, what are you thinking we should give?"

"Well," Gina answered, "Given your pessimistic view of the giving potential of others, I was hoping you would decide to donate the entire $1 million." They all laughed. Charles and Felecia knew that Gina was joking, but even in her humor, Gina had made an impression.

Later that night, the couple realized that what Gina said was true. They really were the people to set the tone for this campaign. Together they decided to give a matching gift of up to $500,000. They would personally match every dollar given, for a total of $1 million. The money was raised, and the food bank's facilities and services were expanded. Through their gift, Charles and Felecia attracted others to support the food bank.

The Lesson

In the midst of all the important work, fund raising is ultimately about people. Enjoy others and enjoy the work. Suggesting that someone give a large sum of money could offend many people. It is certainly not a technique to imitate blindly. But the spirit of Gina's conversation—sincere and engaging—is unbeatable.

Say "I'm Sorry"

The Principle

The only way to entirely avoid making a mistake is to do nothing. Admitting a mistake or misunderstanding, then seeking to repair a relationship affected by that mistake is not an admission of depravity, but of humanity. A timely and sincere apology establishes true character.

Philanthropy is a very human endeavor. When a fund raiser makes a mistake, he should apologize to the donor. A fund raiser should not be afraid to say, "It was my mistake. I will learn from this and do it better next time." Such a response ensures that there will be a next time.

The Story

Neil was the CEO of a major new corporation that was soaring on the stock market. Neil's son, Bryan, attended an independent school. Neil historically provided a modest annual gift to the school. During the previous year, Neil and his wife, Carla, divorced. Neil had weathered the process and was now trying to establish as positive a situation as possible for their child.

One day, Bryan brought home the new school directory. Naturally, Neil flipped through it to verify their information. He was stunned to see that Carla and her new husband, Warren, had received primary listing as Neil's parents, with all the pertinent information: names, numbers, home address, office address, etc.

Neil was hurt, disappointed and mad. He felt that since he paid for Bryan's tuition and other school costs, an indiscretion of this nature should have been caught and corrected by the school administration. But it was not the money that Neil cared about most. What really upset him was realizing how his relationship with Bryan was viewed by the school and then conveyed to everyone else, including his son. Neil was listed as an also-ran, when he knew that he was a vital part of Bryan's life.

There were practical considerations as well. Even though Bryan spent half of his time with Neil, calls and invitations from Bryan's classmates and information about school functions were being directed to Carla's house. Neil, a dedicated father, felt that people would think his son belonged to another man. More importantly, Bryan would soon realize that all his friends only call his mom's home.

These serious personal concerns provided an extraordinary opportunity for school officials to apologize. Unfortunately, the headmaster, Seymour, did not see it that way. To Neil's surprise, Seymour defended the decision to include only one listing. He said that it saved paper and was more efficient. Furthermore, he told Neil that "if the parent had stopped to read the newsletter, he would have known that a preprinted copy of the directory had been available to proof." Of course, Neil would not have received the newsletter due to the school's policy of listing only one parent. Astonished and frustrated, Neil vowed never to make a gift to that school.

Out of love for his son, Neil eventually did give a small gift to the school. However, the director of development, rather than the headmaster, worked with him. The director hoped that Neil would eventually become a major gift contributor. With a simple heartfelt apology from the headmaster, this would have been likely.

The Lesson

Admit mistakes. An apology should be given as soon as the offense becomes obvious. Do not let things simmer. An apology should be sincere, not downplay responsibility, and restitution should be offered whenever possible. Offer to fix it, make it right, and do it better the next time. Nobody likes to make a mistake, but to not admit one compounds the problem.

Success
Breeds
Success

The Principle

Success breeds success. The fund raiser's job is to identify those people whose success will best benefit the institution and then capitalize on the connections.

The Story

A major state university had a board of trustees with a cadre of big names in the community. While each prominent board member had some affiliation to the state university, most had stronger ties with another university or institution either in that state or elsewhere. The vice president, who met privately with each board member, discovered that in the previous five years, fewer than half of the members of the board had made any gifts to the university. Of the 75 board members, not even five had given more than $5,000. Thirty others had given less than $1,000. The remaining board members had given nothing. It was time to make a change.

These board members were all very successful men and women, and no one wanted to offend them. Still, it was important to find those members who were ready to give their time and resources to support the university's efforts. Over time each non-productive board member completed their terms: they were not invited back. Through research and discussion, the vice president identified some key people who were ready for increased involvement. These included the CEO of a new publicly traded company, the chief financial officer (CFO) of a hotel corporation that was going public, the chief counsel of a new food service chain, the CEO of a petroleum company, and an outstanding attorney who stood to inherit substantial sums from her father.

Five years later, every one of the board members had made a gift of at least $100,000 to the university. Virtually two-thirds of the board had donated $500,000 or more, and many gave more than $1 million. It was a board comprised of leaders, as the previous board had been, but now it consisted of leaders who were also financial backers.

The Lesson

Any nonprofit must attract successful individuals who are willing to financially back the institution. If they are not willing to support the institution and cannot be persuaded to change their attitudes toward financial support, find replacements who have zeal and financial commitment.

The Prospects Are Limitless

The Principle

There is enormous wealth in our country today. There are more millionaires than anyone ever imagined who are able to give at greater levels than they ever imagined. Because of this proliferation of wealth, everyone should be viewed as a prospect.

A prospect is not necessarily someone with extravagant wealth. What a prospect must have is a real interest in the agency and the capacity to make a substantial gift. These individuals are not hounded daily for gifts, as are people with more prominent wealth. More than likely, these prospects are seldom asked for anything of significance. They receive mailings, but no one has personally challenged them to consider their role within an institution.

The Story

Harvey spent his entire professional life as an engineer for a state highway department. He and his wife, Phyliss, were childless. The couple enjoyed their time together and were devoted to each other. When Phyliss died unexpectedly, Harvey was lost in grief. Eventually, he began to reach out to others around him. He lived in a retirement community and became the hit of all the social functions. The ladies enjoyed dining, dancing and socializing with Harvey, but his heart belonged to Phyliss.

Harvey became aware that the retirement community's activities were limited due to insufficient transportation. An old bus was available, but it was not reliable. Harvey chose to use the benefits from Phyliss's life insurance policy to purchase a $60,000 bus for the retirement community. Harvey was proud of this contribution, but he never saw it as an act of heroism. It was just his way of helping.

Later, the state's department of health informed the retirement community that it would have to make substantial changes in the center's medical facility or be shut down. The retirement community planners had been saving money for a full-service medical facility, but they did not have enough. So they initiated a major campaign to raise $6 million for the new building.

Harvey had been a good steward over the years and was comfortable financially. He felt that Phyliss would have wanted him to support this retirement community. When Maria, a retirement community development officer, asked if Harvey would like to make a gift in honor of Phyliss, he heartily agreed. He invested $1 million in the campaign with the understanding that Phyliss' name would be on this medical facility.

Today, the medical building prominently displays Phyliss' name—a testimony to her life and to Harvey's great love for his wife. Shortly after making this gift, Harvey became very ill and died, but many people have continued to benefit from Harvey's generosity.

The Lesson

Prospects are everywhere. Treat everyone as if he or she could be the agency's next donor.

Earn Trust

The Principle

The more a donor trusts a fund raiser, the better the opportunity for a successful gift solicitation. Donors often say, "The reason I am going to make this gift is because I trust you."

The Story

Several years ago, Stuart, a fund raiser, participated in the creation of a contractual arrangement between a theater and one of its donors, Millie. The theater's leaders agreed to recognize the donor in the naming of the newly renovated facility. In turn, Millie and Mark gave $500,000. She genuinely appreciated the opportunity to make the gift and gave it with great affection.

As part of the contractual arrangement, the theater's leaders agreed that the theater would annually run a picture of the donors with accompanying biographical information about them in at least one of the theater's production programs. An additional requirement said that the formal name of the theater, which included the donors' names, be used in all publications.

Eventually, Millie and Mark passed away. Stuart might have considered his obligation to Millie fulfilled, but he did not. Stuart felt responsible to see that the agreements made with Millie were upheld. He regularly monitored the theater's programs to see if her picture and biographical information were still included at least once annually. Any time a new executive director failed to realize the nature of the agreement with Millie, Stuart was there to remind him.

The Lesson

Fund raisers have a responsibility to see to it that their institutions follow through on commitments. Trust can never be donated. It must always be earned.

Use the Tools, But Keep It Personal

The Principle

Advanced technology in the field of fund raising has paved the way for great progress, yet much has been lost. Literature and training programs for development officers usually emphasize the technical aspect of the work and neglect the human dimension. This results in an unbalanced view of philanthropy.

Fund-raising organizations now commission consulting firms to do prospect evaluations and appraisals. These tools are helpful, but they are still just tools. Fund raisers who master the technology, without letting it control their efforts, accomplish the most success-ful solicitations. The most accurate evaluations are still performed face-to-face. Fund raisers who depend on technology may be tempted to listen less intently, because they assume they already have the facts.

People are not demographics. They are constantly changing and unpredictable. Only through disciplined listening will a fund raiser be able to respond to the donor's concerns. Empathy from the fund raiser often elicits a reciprocal concern from the donor. This give and take cannot be generated by a computer.

The Story

A planned-gift officer for an art museum approached George, a real estate mogul, about contributing one of his buildings, worth more than $1 million. The officer explained to George that this gift would only cost him $10,000. But George did not want to give away $10,000. This was not surprising and no gift resulted.

The planned-gift officer paid more attention to his technique than to whether or not George was interested in supporting the project. Under different conditions, the ability to give so large a gift for so little cash might have appealed to George. The planned-gift officer failed to discover George's interests and facilitate his desire to give. No donor is thrilled by the mere presentation of the mechanical aspects of giving.

The Lesson

Use the available technology, but do not skimp on personal research. Treat the donors as the unique individuals they are. Treat the project with more affection than the plan to accomplish it. Be an artisan, not a hardware salesman. Capture the donor's imagination before rolling out the blueprint.

Be Confident, Not Arrogant

The Principle

True confidence is contagious. A fund raiser who authentically supports an agency and is genuinely self-assured is a powerful draw for a financial campaign.

An arrogant fund raiser, however, can have the opposite effect actually discouraging the donor from giving. Because the fund raiser reflects directly upon the institution that employs her, donors may feel that under the circumstances, their philanthropy would be better served elsewhere.

The fund raiser's demeanor can either warm or chill the prospective donor and affect any ensuing gift. If a fund raiser is self-absorbed rather than conscious of the donor's needs, this will probably be her undoing. Fund-raisers who come across as arrogant are viewed as indecorous.

One who is equipped with thorough research and expertise in the area of solicitation exudes confidence and ability in style and presentation. This allows the fund raiser to be at ease during the solicitation process. Confidence is authentic and always in good taste. Arrogance is artificial and leaves a bad impression.

The Story

A major corporation with branches scattered across the nation had a branch in Kevin's hometown. Kevin, a development director, and

Melissa, his chief executive officer, visited the local plant to meet with the plant manager, John to ask him for a $5 million gift from the company. A strong relationship already existed between the agency and the plant. In fact, the plant manager had previously indicated that a significant gift was possible and that he would do all he could to make such a gift.

After hearing the proposal, John felt that the amount requested exceeded his company's financial capabilities. He remarked, "This corporation has never made a gift at that level." In spite of John's initial reaction, Kevin remained steadfast. His confidence was based on solid and thorough research. Kevin reached into his briefcase and pulled out a newspaper clipping heralding a gift of more than $10 million that John's company had made to a similar project in its headquarters' city.

Because Kevin was confident and prepared, he convincingly advocated his position. He gave the plant manager a compelling case to present to those who would make the final gift-giving decision. Although the company did not give the entire $5 million, they did give $2.5 million, the largest gift ever given by this company to any agency in Kevin's community.

The Lesson

Preparation results in justifiable confidence. Do the necessary research to be sure of the appropriateness of the solicitation request. Do not rely on the smoke and mirrors of self-promotion. The road to fund-raising success is littered with the unrealized potential of arrogant fund raisers.

It Takes a Team

The Principle

On an organizational chart, the development officer may appear to be the key to fund raising. But the development director cannot do it alone.

Often those handling the daily program or administrative responsibilities of an agency can best convey to donors the importance of a project. Staff members can sometimes share the dreams and visions of a program in a way that captures the imagination of a prospective donor.

It is important to recognize that receiving a gift is the result of team effort. Usually, others are involved in the process leading up to solicitation—identifying prospects, doing research, and cultivating relationships. Their impassioned commitment to the organization sends a message to a prospective donor that transcends formal presentations.

The Story

The children's center is a live-in facility where the courts can refer children who, for various reasons, need assistance. The nature of these children requires that the staff give much effort and energy to their work.

One day the center was preparing for a visit by Betty, the president of a major foundation. Bill, the children center's vice president of development, invited Betty to have lunch at the campus, tour the facilities and discuss the program. Obviously, he anticipated the opportunity to solicit a substantial gift for the center's continued work.

Bill invited Marsha, the center's director of programs, to join them for the campus tour. Prior to Betty's arrival, Marsha warned Bill of a problem. The previous night a young resident had extensively damaged the cottage that Bill planned to visit on the tour. The maintenance team had not had time to clean and restore the cottage.

Bill and Marsha agreed that it would be best to exclude this cottage from the scheduled tour, and they looked for a different cottage to highlight. During the tour, they told Betty about the substitution. To their surprise, she specifically requested to see that cottage. Betty felt it was important to see exactly what the staff at the center dealt with day in and day out.

Following the tour, Betty walked toward her car, discussing with Marsha the issues surrounding the angry young resident who had torn up the cottage. Arriving at the car, Betty told Marsha, "You take care of the young people here, and we'll make sure you have enough money. Thank you for giving me a chance to help."

On that day a relationship began with a gift of more than $100,000. Every year since, her gifts to that agency have ranged from $50,000 to $200,000 in support of the ongoing work with children. Now, with gifts totaling more than a million dollars, this represents the good work done by program staff.

The Lesson

In every agency key individuals exist who make that program what it is. At an art museum, it may be the curator. At a retirement home, it may be the director of activities or the head of nursing. At a hospital, it may be the chief of medical services or a head nurse. At a university, it may be a member of the faculty or a housemother.

Whatever the institution, the staff often best demonstrates how gifts are being used. They can make the difference.

How Committed Are the "Owners"?

The Principle

In a sole proprietorship, the buck stops with one soul. In a partnership, at least two necks are on the line. In a large company, a president or chief executive officer sets the course and leads the way. But who really "owns" a nonprofit organization? It is, in fact, the volunteer board.

A deep commitment from board members is critical to any fundraising effort. If a board member believes in the mission of an institution, his actions show it. Prospective donors are naturally interested in whether board members are deeply committed to their cause. Plainly stated, have the board members put their money where their mouths are? If those most involved are not giving, it is unlikely that a prospect will feel compelled to give.

The Story

A ballet company asked Anna for a million-dollar gift. Initially, she was flattered and a bit overwhelmed that they believed she could make such a gift. She certainly cared and wanted to be a part of the ballet company's advancement.

Before committing to a gift, Anna asked a few questions. Her first request was, "Tell me about your board of directors." Jane, the executive director, told her about the fine men and women who served on the board for the ballet, some of whom Anna knew. Probing further, Anna asked, "What is your board's financial commitment to this fund-raising effort?" Jane explained that the ballets board was not a fund-raising board but was a "hands-on, hard-working" board.

Anna replied, "Well, it takes a whole lot of work to make a million dollars." While the board members might be well-meaning and committed to the agency, this commitment obviously did not extend to financial support. Anna felt that financial sacrifice was a legitimate way for the board members to show the extent of their commitment to the ballet. The ballet lost the opportunity for Anna's million-dollar gift.

Anna went on to donate several million-dollar gifts to other agencies in her lifetime. The board members of these agencies may never have matched the size of her donations; however, the board members' gifts were comparable in terms of the sacrifice represented. Anna felt this demonstrated true commitment.

The Lesson

Donors expect board members and other people with "ownership" to demonstrate their commitment not only in words, but also with dollars.

Church For The Heart of The City

Grace & Holy Trinity Cathedral

A church known as the "Church for the Heart of the City" ran into a problem in the early 1990s: the 105-year-old Grace and Holy Trinity Cathedral was running out of space.

Founded in 1894, the Church—which has a legacy of service to the community—was originally located in the old Grace Church. Later the church embarked on a plan to build a larger church and parish house.

Trinity Church voted in 1912 to merge with Grace Church to become the Grace and Holy Trinity. In 1935, Grace and Holy Trinity was officially declared a Cathedral by Bishop Robert Nelson Spencer.

Through the years, the church added space and renovated existing buildings to continue the cathedral's ministry. Haden Hall was constructed in 1954 to provide space for education and community service, and in 1960 renovations were completed to the old parish house.

The church suffered a substantial setback in 1986, when the north wall of the cathedral crashed down. Services were held in Haden Hall for 20 months. At that time, the church had the opportunity to sell its valuable land and move to the suburbs. Instead, the vestry, the clergy, the wardens and the congregation were determined to remain the "Church for the Heart of the City."

The First Steps

In the early 1990s, the church once again faced a decision: how to raise funds to add additional space to expand its outreach efforts. Plans were set in motion for a Founder's Hall. Only a vision in 1992, it is becoming a reality at the Cathedral campus.

The $4 million building opens up 18,000 square feet of space for social, educational and community service needs.

"The goal of Founders' Hall is to be a facility of ministry not only for our congregation, but also for our city, our Diocese, the larger church and the poor," said The Very Reverend Dennis J. J. Schmidt, Dean of the Cathedral.

The project began with a $2 million donation from the W. T. Kemper Trust at Commerce Bank, a $500,000 Founders' Gift and a $32,000 Cornerstone Gift. Efforts to raise an additional $2 million concentrated heavily on the historic church's 1,200-member congregation. Nearly 215 gifts comprise the $4,850,000 project total.

Project Summary

In 1992, the dean of the cathedral recognized that growth in new families and ministries required expanded facilities. He appointed a Planning and Building Committee to explore and implement the project. Of primary concern were the cathedral's continued ministry of outreach and service, additional educational facilities and added meeting space.

A master plan analyzed facility needs and determined an additional 18,000 square feet of space was needed. A building plan was developed that would double the size of the Community Kitchen, an outreach service that feeds about 300 homeless and poor people daily. The expanded kitchen was located on the ground level for accessibility. A multipurpose room was added for counseling and a work training project.

The plan also included an upper courtyard level which contained three meeting rooms, a 3,140-square-foot social hall and kitchen. The area is suitable for receptions, music, theatrical productions and public events. An outside courtyard for recitals, seminars, banquets and presentations was also included. The courtyard, with surrounding garden, was designed to seat up to 400 guests.

The Campaign

The Hartsook firm, was retained to assist with the capital campaign. A 12-member committee was led by Mary Shaw Branton, Richard Fanolio and Albert Mauro, Sr.

"The firm was instrumental in helping to set a campaign goal, establish a campaign strategy and identify potential donors," said Dean Schmidt. "They also did an initial market test by interviewing people regarding the project and their interest. They helped prepare literature, plan strategies and assist with the overall campaign."

"The firm's leadership, combined with strong support of the church congregation and community, were two factors that eventually led to fund-raising success," he added. "We definitely would not have been this successful without Hartsook. They helped us prioritize and set goals. They screened potential donors and gave us sound advice. They attended our monthly campaign committee meetings and advised us on what steps to take next."

Donations and Memorial Gifts

Because the campaign focused on church members' gifts, the campaign committee identified a variety of ways members could support the building project.

Gifts could be made in cash, pledges, marketable securities, closely-held securities, tangible personal property, real estate, corporate matching gifts, gifts in kind and charitable lead trusts.

Individual gifts were solicited in six categories: Founders' Gifts, $500,000 and above; Benefactors' Gifts, $250,000 to $499,999; Sponsors' Gifts, $100,000 to $249,999; Sustainers' Gifts, $25,000 to $99,999; Cornerstone Gifts $5,000 to $24,999; and Supporting Gifts, up to $4,999.

All gifts to the campaign could be designated as gifts "in memory" or "in thanksgiving" of loved ones. Additionally, Founders', Benefactors' and Sponsors' names would be inscribed on the court-yard colonnade or in the garden, and opportunities were made for named gifts, such as windows, colonnades, rooms and gardens.

All campaign donors were also notified that they would be recog-nized in the *Angelus*, the cathedral's annual report, as well as in the official campaign report and the Cathedral Memorial Book.

The Results

The campaign committee reached its goal and work has now been completed on the project.

Dean Schmidt said the result is that the parish will not only contin-ue its legacy of community outreach but will expand its services to reach even more members of the community.

"The parish must grow and the parish must continue to serve and serve more largely than it is now," he said. "By expanding, we are making sure that we will reach beyond the present and are insuring our future at the heart of Kansas City and the heartland of America."

Nobody
Else Will
Unless
You Do!

It's There For the Asking

The Principle

Since 1949 (the year philanthropy records were first kept), little growth has occurred in charitable giving. This lack of growth can be attributed to fund raisers who lack aggressiveness, adequate research and proper preparation for the solicitation process.

The Story

Nearly everyone remembers Ted Turner's $1 billion gift to the United Nations in late 1997. What many may have not considered is that this was an unsolicited gift. While we can celebrate his philanthropic example, it raises a disturbing question—how many other dormant gifts are there? Do not assume that everyone with the means to give will do so without being asked.

Furthermore, asking is not enough. Donors must be asked intelligently since solicitation without ample preparation and cultivation is presumptuous. In addition, cultivation of a donor without clear identification is clumsy. Sound research, solid relationships, and intelligent requests produce splendid results.

People who believe that the amount of money available is limited to certain finite amounts miss the point. Lack of wealth is not the enemy. The only thing holding back a greater flow of philan-thropic dollars is the lack of fund raisers willing to give the neces-sary time and energy to become properly prepared.

The Lesson

A gift not solicited is usually a gift not received. Do not sit around waiting for a gift such as Ted Turner's to come along. Saddle up and go find it.

Don't Talk Past the Money

The Principle

It is better to say too little than too much. The solicitation process can be very exciting. Anxiety can easily build up, and the fund raiser may not realize how much adrenaline is flowing. This happens to veterans as well as rookies.

Compensate for overeagerness. The risk is that in the flow of enthusiasm, a fund raiser may be swept away by the excitement and talk right past the money. The donor can become worn out from the intensity of emotion and the onslaught of words. By the time the solicitation finally comes, the donor may be more eager to get out of there than to talk about a giving opportunity.

On the other hand, the time will come when a fund raiser loses his intensity and enthusiasm. Years of saying the same thing over and over and repeating the same stories can cause a person to shift into autopilot and talk beyond the interest of the donor without listening for spontaneous and unspoken responses from the donor.

The Story

Perry is a wonderful man, dedicated to the school where he served as the head of its local foundation for many years. He had raised substantial funds for the school and had worked very hard, but over the years he had grown tired. He had told the same stories so many times that he was numb to their impact.

At a meeting with Lawrence, an alumnus, Perry was recounting another story, unaware of Lawrence's minor impatience. Finally, Lawrence interjected, "Perry, what is it that you want?"

Startled from his monologue, Perry answered, "Well, we just wanted you to know how much you are appreciated."

"OK. Now what else do you want?" Lawrence pressed.

Surprised again, Perry just stared for a second. Lawrence continued, "Do you want a gift?"

"Well, yes, of course we do. Whatever you feel you can give," Perry finally responded. Larry made arrangements for a gift of $25,000 to be given to his alma mater. But he was acutely aware that Perry lacked the enthusiasm necessary to listen and respond to a prospective donor.

The Lesson

Somewhere between nervous energy and bored lethargy is a safe place for solicitation. Check your pulse and make sure you have one, but also make sure it is not racing past the donor's level of participation. Say what you need to, but as you do, listen to the donor—even if the donor is not talking.

The Magic Number Is Three

The Principle

The solicitation of a major gift should never be done by mail. However, after the personal solicitation, the donor should receive a simple letter outlining the provisions of the request. The letter should be straightforward and strategic. With solicitation letters, "less is more."

The Story

Ralph is the senior vice president of fund raising for the Fellowship of Christian Athletes (FCA). After attending a fund-raising seminar, Ralph made a change in the way the organization solicited donors. The change was to include a short and concise letter identifying every solicitation request made. Following a major national campaign, the organization reported incredible success due in part to this simple change.

The letter on a single sheet of paper was drafted in accordance with the following:

1. The first paragraph should say, "We like you, and you like us" (or something to that effect). Most organizations usually add a little more to this paragraph.

2. The second paragraph should spell out the terms of the proposed agreement. "We wish for you to consider a gift of $1 million, payable over a five-year period, in which you set the timing of each payment. For this we would be honored to recognize you, or a member of your family, or a person that you designate, by adding that name to our new building."

3. The third paragraph should complete the letter with, "We still really like you and hope you still like us."

According to Ralph, this simple letter was an important tool for the FCA as it moved forward in its major national campaign.

The Lesson

By the time a leadership gift is solicited, big brochures, fast-paced films, and glitzy presentations are too much, too late. A simple, clean letter is much more effective. It respects the donor's relationship with the organization and affirms that the donor is already part of the important work—an insider. Keep it simple.

Show, Don't Just Tell

The Principle

A prominent man in the cable television industry said that when he was first introduced to what the cable business could accomplish, he found a way for the product to sell itself. All he needed to do was set up his equipment in an appropriate location some distance from a major community. He would plug the cable equipment into a television set and bring people in to watch. After that, he simply had to tell prospective customers how they could have television access in their own homes.

Now a billionaire, this man's insight still remains good advice: "A presentation without a demonstration is merely a conversation." Many organizations and institutions successfully solicit gifts because fund raisers have learned how to show, rather than merely tell, what a gift could accomplish.

The Story

Ralph and Natalie cared a great deal about their family members, especially Ralph's mother who lived at a local retirement community. They valued the quality care that she received. Sid, the director of development told Ralph and Natalie about a benevolent fund at the center which allowed anyone living at the center to receive care regardless of ability to pay. Sid—without naming the persons—told of a man who had used all his resources to enter contests. He had gone through $400,000. Foolish, yes, but he was drawn in by the promise of greater riches. They also learned of a man who would use all of his resources to support his wife in her fight against cancer. Ralph and Natalie were moved.

Shortly after the death of Ralph's mother, the couple were told by Sid of several residents who had run out of resources and were dependent on the retirement center's benevolent fund. Ralph and Natalie were seeing firsthand the impact that giving had on the retirement community. Sid asked them to remember Ralph's mother with a gift. They gave a $2 million endowment to support in perpetuity the benevolent mission of the retirement center.

The Lesson

Show donors how their gifts can be used. Don't rely on words alone. A picture (or other demonstration) is worth more than a thousand words—maybe even a million dollars.

Ask For a Specific Amount

The Principle

When you ask a donor for a gift, you have expectations about the size of that gift. If this amount is never mentioned, how can the donor be expected to give at that level?

The Story

Norma, who was very interested in making an important gift to her alma mater, was solicited for a gift of $12 to $15 million. The university's foundation officers knew she could make a $12 million gift and thought as much as $15 million was possible. They were afraid to take the leap and unwilling to spend the extra time for the cultivation that might have made them more confident in requesting the higher amount.

By their actions, the foundation officers implied that the university would be as pleased with $12 million as $15 million. To her credit, Norma donated $12 million, which was an important gift that expressed her commitment.

But the foundation officers left $3 million on the table.

The Lesson

When a gift range is suggested, the donor typically gives the minimum suggested. It is better to ask for a specific amount in a confident and dignified way that does not demean the fund raiser and expresses respect and appreciation for the donor.

Jerry Doesn't Raise All That Money That Weekend

The Principle

Every Labor Day, Jerry Lewis conducts his annual telethon to support the fight against muscular dystrophy. An enormous amount of money is raised—millions of dollars donated toward research and support. It is tempting to see this success and to hope for the same kind of results in a similar amount of time. Unfortunately, no matter how worthwhile the cause, and no matter how attractive the medium, very little can be done in a weekend (or even in a month of weekends).

For Jerry's Kids, as for all successful fund-raising efforts, the real work happens deliberately, behind the scenes, over long periods of time. The outcome of the Labor Day telethon is not a result of the activities of just that weekend. The relatively few individuals handing over huge checks to Jerry and his associates actually represent thousands of hours worked, planned and invested all year long. There are no quick or effortless ways to accomplish a fund-raising goal.

The Story

An agency supporting abused children had a need for a new campus facility within the city, relocating from the suburbs to a more accessible location. In their enthusiasm, those in charge of the agency believed that they needed only to make the community aware of their plight. In order to get the word out, the leaders publicly announced a major fund-raising drive, hoping to raise several million dollars to purchase land and build the new facility. Having announced their plans, they waited for a response from the community. They waited and waited, but no money arrived.

Despite the initial zeal, the children's agency had neither organization nor leadership in the area of fund raising. The agency had a nice article in the newspaper but no money. Eventually, the options on the purchase of land expired. Discouraged, the agency's leaders abandoned the project.

A year later, for reasons known only to themselves, the agency leaders announced the project once again. This attempt also ended in failure. Again, the contract to buy downtown property lapsed.

Finally, the agency's leadership decided to try something different. Certainly, the new facility was a genuine need. However, the need alone did not satisfy the fund-raising goal. Consequently, they hired a fund raiser to help achieve the campaign's goal. The fund raiser conducted thorough research, identified prospects and mapped out a strategy for attaining the goal.

Rather than starting with an announcement, the children's agency asked for money quietly and privately. Through this patient, purposeful endeavor, a substantial sum was committed. Once the agency reached 90 percent of its goal, the leadership again publicly announced the fund-raising campaign. Previously, the community had responded with cynicism due to the institution's premature announcements. However, with just ten percent yet to raise, tremendous confidence surrounded the campaign.

The Lesson

Wishful thinking will not fulfill a goal. Sparkling press announcements will not bring success. Careful planning and quiet networking will bring about successful fund raising.

Inspire Others To Give

The Principle

Every donor, particularly a person who makes a large gift, has an opportunity to make a second gift. This second gift is one of affiliation. The willingness of a donor to be publicly affiliated with an institution helps others to have confidence in that institution. This is an important commitment for a donor and should not be taken lightly.

By publicly associating with an institution, donors offer something of much greater value than money—their names and reputations. Building a solid reputation, especially in this day and age, is harder than building a strong financial portfolio.

While public recognition can have a tremendous upside, it can also create concerns. Once donors are seen as philanthropists, they will be solicited by many other agencies. This can be time-consuming and annoying. More importantly, there may be some safety concerns for the donor and the donor's family in being publicly recognized as having substantial wealth. Finally, any further actions of the agency automatically become associated with this individual.

Although normally a positive opportunity, public association with an institution still represents a step of faith on the part of the donor. For these reasons, the second gift of affiliation should not be taken for granted. When a donor chooses to be involved in this manner, it is a great privilege.

The Story

Kathy and Pete gave a million dollars to the YWCA. Kathy was an active volunteer with the YWCA in her community and believed strongly in its work. She and Pete, who served as board chair of a major national corporation, also decided to contribute appreciated stock. That public display of support had an even more positive impact on the YWCA within the community than the initial million-dollar gift.

Although these gifts were very generous, they did not compare in value to the public affiliation that this family gave to the YWCA. This couple's involvement raised the credibility of the organization, as well as the level of respect that the YWCA received from other funding sources.

The Lesson

Encourage donors to allow some level of recognition or affiliation, not only as an opportunity to personally recognize them, but also for its benefit to the agency. This should be offered as an opportunity to make an additional gift, acknowledging the commitment and sacrifice involved.

Sit on The Donor's Side of The Table

The Principle

A fund raiser should be acutely aware of the agency's needs. She should have a clear view and very personal perspective on how she would like things to be arranged. If a fund raiser were free to order anything from the gift-giving menu, she would know exactly what items to order and how she would like them served.

But this kind of carte blanche encounter is rarely, encountered. In reality, a fund raiser must focus on the donor's personal preferences and needs. An effective fund raiser will quickly come around to the donor's side of the table to make the appeal.

A solicitation that considers the needs, desires, concerns and dreams of the donor will likely be filled at a much higher level than one that neglects these issues. A fund raiser who genuinely wants to fulfill the expectations of a philanthropist sets aside personal preferences and instead looks at things from the donor's perspective.

The Story

Ruth and Milton owned a business in the same neighborhood as their favorite hospital. When their business sold, the new owners moved out of Ruth and Milton's building (the building was not sold as part of the sale of the business. Because of its location, Ruth and Milton approached the hospital about renting space. The hospital, a major landowner in the area, suggested that the couple consider various ways they might gift the building.

Reluctantly, they agreed. When meeting with Tom, the planned gift officer for the hospital, it was clear that an outright transfer of ownership was not practical. Ruth and Milton, while having a tax need, also needed the income either from the sale of the building or the renting of the space. Understanding their needs, Tom suggested a trust that would give them a lifetime income if they were willing to give the building to the hospital's foundation. The building had an appraised value of $1.8 million and the foundation was willing to give Ruth and Milton a ten percent annual payment. That $180,000 a year would even have some tax free components. The payments would go on for the remainder of their lives. Both were in their mid to late 60s. The deal was made. The hospital then rented space from the foundation, giving the foundation the income to pay the gift trust payment annually.

Because Tom was on Ruth and Milton's side of the table, he found a way to meet their needs as well as those of the foundation.

The Lesson

A fund raiser benefits from first identifying the donor's needs and then owning them. This approach not only overcomes donor reticence, it liberates the donor to give larger gifts. A donor who senses that the fund raiser has taken the role of advocate can relax and throw himself into the mission of the agency. Working from the same side of the table, both the donor and the fund raiser can leave satisfied.

Recognize Personal Achievement

The Principle

A donor may feel that due to his own achievements, he is now in a financial position to give back to those who have given to him.

The Story

After a lifetime of successful endeavors, Tom felt that it was time to thank and recognize his university which he had attended for only a year. He wanted others to understand and appreciate the values demonstrated by this university. Tom also wanted to create some lasting recognition for his successful business career.

Tom's gift of several million dollars allowed the university to erect a building and establish an endowment.

The Lesson

Consider those who have attained some level of personal success. Encourage them to make gifts recognizing personal achievements and expressing appreciation.

Don't Jump The Gun

The Principle

One of the common miscalculations of philanthropy is to ask too soon. The fund raiser's mantra, "There is no gift if you do not ask," permeates philanthropy to the extent that it overshadows other equally important considerations such as the less-quoted maxim, "Nobody wants to give money away."

How can these be reconciled? Actually, they merge beautifully when a prospect has developed an affinity for a project, a fondness for an agency and associated individuals, and confidence that his money can improve things. When a donor believes that people will be helped and that lives will be enriched, he views his gift not as a give-away, but as an investment. Then, and only then, is it appropriate to ask a donor to consider making a gift.

The Story

Mary was a supporter of the local art museum. She loved art and visited the museum often over the years. While she was still working it was impossible for her to donate much time or money. After retiring and receiving an inheritance, she had some discretionary time and resources. Staff at the museum noticed that Mary now showed up to volunteer, and they had also heard of her inheritance. To some eager fund raisers, this looked like kismet.

Inviting Mary to lunch, the museum representatives immediately solicited a gift. They detailed a new exhibit program that the museum officials wanted to develop and asked her for $100,000. Mary looked at them and answered, "While it is true that I've enjoyed this museum, I really don't know that much about you or the museum." Specifically, she questioned the direction of the museum and its purpose, goals and details concerning the new exhibit program.

The fund raisers had not prepared Mary for this opportunity, and she was not ready to give her money away.

Hearing about the solicitation, Wanda, the board chair of the museum, called Mary and took her out to lunch again. Wanda knew Mary and realized that Mary needed a greater understanding and appreciation of the museum's plans before making a gift. Wanda apologized for the premature solicitation and the rudeness that it conveyed. Instead of asking Mary for money, Wanda encouraged Mary by answering questions and providing more information about the museum. Mary gained a greater understanding of the museum's operation and vision for the future.

Mary enjoyed that conversation and a subsequent small group discussion. She was invited to participate in an area focus group on the image and role of the museum in the community. Months later Mary was asked to sponsor a smaller program that required a gift of $5,000. She readily agreed.

Mary attended that exhibit opening and several others. Soon she was asked to serve on an important task force to direct long-term planning. She quickly became one of its most active participants, a vocal and ardent supporter. Three years later Mary gave more than $1 million to the museum and included the museum in her estate plan a gift with a value of several million dollars.

That premature solicitation could have ended an important and valued relationship. Wanda's patience, support and cultivation saved the day and resulted in a wonderful gift for the museum.

The Lesson

We need to know who our donors are and what they envision. A donor's money does not immediately qualify for a fund-raising solicitation.

Trust Is a Two-Way Street

The Principle

There is great concern today regarding the legal aspects of any endeavor. Reading the fine print has become an American pastime. Philanthropy has not been spared this litigious mood, which often extends to the legalities surrounding a pledge or commitment. In spite of these legal concerns, donors expect trust regarding their commitments. Fund raisers cannot allow relationships with donors to become adversarial.

The Story

Melvin, the director of development at a retirement community, witnessed daily the effects of aging and the resulting need for quality care facilities. Melvin's responsibility was to cultivate and solicit residents for gifts that would benefit the retirement community. Two projects in particular interested Melvin and captured the attention of the residents. One was an activity facility with provisions for crafts and woodworking, and the other was a benevolent fund to assist residents whose financial resources were exhausted.

One day Melvin visited Jean, a resident of the retirement community. Jean, who never had children, worked hard in her professional career and chose the retirement community to make sure she received care in her advancing years. She had little interest in crafts or activities but enjoyed sitting on the balcony watching others as they passed by or participated in activities. She had seen how the crafts and activities, such as exercises at the therapeutic pool, had benefitted others. People seemed energized as a result of their activity.

While not extremely wealthy, Jean was blessed with a small inheritance and had accumulated modest funds. Melvin knew of her relative affluence and asked her to consider making a lead gift that would initiate confidence regarding the creation of a crafts and wood shop center. Melvin asked for $250,000 and let Jean know that this could be given over time, at her own pace. Jean said that whenever she gave a gift, it was always as a one-time payment because she did not know whether she would be around to finish the pledge. Melvin asked if she was willing to make this kind of commitment. "Yes," she answered, "I'm inclined to do that."

Leaders in the project had impressed upon Melvin that he had to seal a commitment with a pledge card. Melvin agreed this would move the prospect closer to the actual gift and result in a greater sense of commitment. He asked Jean if she would please sign a card indicating their agreement, which he would submit to the executive director. Jean was astonished. She asked, "You mean you need a piece of paper to believe that I will do what I just said I was going to do?"

Melvin was caught off guard. He responded, "It is not for me, Jean. It is what the board wants." Jean answered, "If that is what other people want, they are not going to get it from me. If you do not trust me to do what I have said, then I do not know how I can trust you to do what you have said." Jean did not make that gift and the project floundered.

The Lesson

Know your donor and give her room to work within her comfort zone. Be aware of what might cross that line for her emotionally. Listen and respond carefully, rather than trying to take a strong lead. Grabbing the bull by the horns may be good for bulls, but leading with affection, trust and encouragement is more appropriate for philanthropy.

Handle With Care

The Principle

If a fund raiser follows all of the right strategies and the donor still declines the solicitation, there may be a more personal explanation. Perhaps prospective donors have been properly identified as caring about the agency and would usually have the capacity to give but are unable to do so at that time. These situations could be as unique as the institutionalization of a child, a severe medical setback of a parent or embezzlement within a company, or they could be as common as a business reversal. When a properly identified prospect shares this kind of intimate information along with their regrets, this is a qualified "no."

The positive side of this encounter is that good research has produced an accurate identification of a prospect. The downside is that the timing is not right for an immediate significant gift.

A qualified "no" is something to handle with delicacy and great care. Do not take lightly what has been shared. At the next encounter, be sure to ask how things are going, not as a means to an end but from genuine concern. This demonstrates that the prospective donors are remembered and still seen as having a potential role in the future. Ask the donors questions about things that matter to them, such as, "How is your child?" "How are your parents doing?" "How is your business?" These questions show an awareness of the donors' personal concerns and can provide a good foundation for a growing relationship.

The Story

Tim and his wife, Violet, owned a thriving telemarketing company with a large number of phone banks. Their business distributed dry goods across the nation, and the couple owned warehouses all over the country to store and distribute their products. Tim and Violet were smart, hard working and committed to the arts.

This couple served on an advisory board for a new continuing education facility in the arts. When Dana, the vice president for development, asked them for a $1 million commitment toward the program, they had every reason to want to help. Despite the couple's high interest and apparent ability to give, Tim responded, "We believe in what you are doing, and we support the work. However, our auditors recently discovered that one of our account managers has been padding the inventory receipts and selling off merchandise. Our loss amounts to several million dollars. Until we get this worked out, Violet and I are not in a position to make a gift. We are sorry."

Obviously Dana was disappointed. Still, she let them know that she understood. She encouraged them in the belief that it would all be resolved and that things would be set right in time. Two years later, the manager was arrested and sentenced to serve time and pay restitution. Although they had little hope of recovering this money, Tim and Violet felt that the issue was resolved. They were ready to make a commitment to the arts program, which was still very important to them. Although the couple had been unable to kick off the campaign, their gift of $1 million sealed its success.

The Lesson

A qualified "no" is preferred over a perfunctory "no." A perfunctory "no" means "We do not have it in our budget" or "We are not really interested in your project." At this level of fund raising, proper identification should rule out the possibility of receiving a perfunctory "no." However, a qualified "no" says the solicitation was on the right track, but unexpected circumstances were inhibiting the gift. Do not cross these people off the list. Continue to reach out with appropriate concern and friendship.

What's In a Name?

The Principle

One reason people give is to recognize the works and efforts of another. This is an excellent opportunity for an agency to offer a donor the possibility of name recognition.

The Story

The Hale family believed in and deeply appreciated the work of a former headmaster of a private school. The Hale family also valued the role this school had played in the life of each family member. In an effort to rebuild the entire campus, the Hale's became one of the principal backers of the project. During a capital campaign, they donated $3 million toward a new middle school building. This became a great opportunity to recognize the former headmaster. This gift, with the opportunity to name the building on the headmasters behalf, honored the headmaster for his years of devoted work and effort. It also honored the Hales for their character.

The Lesson

Consider offering the donor an opportunity to name a project. Is there an individual who has greatly influenced the donor? Is there a

person the donor would like to honor? Some donors find this a powerful incentive toward project involvement.

Never Tell
A Donor
What
To Give

The Principle

"I am not going to be told what to give."

"No one is going to dictate my financial decisions."

Some fund raisers hear these kinds of remarks from prospects. Fund raisers should never tell a prospect what level of gift to make. Instead, fund raisers should ask a donor to consider a gift at a certain level. By suggesting a specific amount, the donor can better appreciate what is needed for the project to be a success.

The Story

Once on a business flight, Bob had a conversation with Jeff, the head of a large corporation. Jeff explained that he loved his job, but he did not enjoy the public side of raising money on behalf of the corporation. He hated going into a place and saying, "Our corporation is giving away a million dollars, and you should too." Jeff further confided, "It makes me feel very uncomfortable because it is their money, and they should be the ones deciding how to spend it." He had continued to fulfill this aspect of his job only because he felt that it was expected of him.

Jeff was surprised and relieved by Bob's response. "Jeff, you are wrong. That is not what is expected of you. Many people do it that way, and some have limited success, but I feel that those tactics will not work for long. I hope that more people will come with an attitude that says, 'We believe in this work $1 million worth, and we hope you will consider making a similar gift.'"

This less demanding posture liberates people to make a positive decision. Without the pressure, they are free to listen and be carried away with the opportunity to be involved in an important work—moved to give, rather than being put off by pushiness.

The Lesson

No one owes a gift to any agency. Therefore, no one should demand participation. On parting, Bob gave Jeff a copy of a book, *Closing That Gift!* Bob inscribed the book with, "Never demand. Only ask." That is still the message.

Your Greatest Competition Is Not the Competition

The Principle

Struggles for superiority distract an agency from its purpose. One children's agency might compare its work with another agency in order to highlight its own strong points. Or an environmental group might compare its work with another environmental group.

And negative comparisons can be self-defeating. Church members might remark, "We just cannot achieve the campaign success of that other church."

The struggle against superiority or self-defeat can occur within any group—a retirement home or a theater, a hospital or a university. No one is immune to the comparison trap. In actuality, each entity is so unique that success or failure rests solely on an agency's own performance.

More than enough wealth is available. In the United States, money donated toward philanthropic efforts has never exceeded two percent of the country's gross domestic product. The fund raiser's job is to bring the agency to the attention of the right people and offer an appropriate message. With proper representation, an organization's name becomes synonymous with character, competence, and concern for people.

The Story

Myra had been a long-time supporter of her local hospital. She regularly donated small gifts and was an auxiliary volunteer. She also supported the hospital's various fund-raising event ventures such as runs and T-shirt sales. But, it was not until Myra's best friend, Judy, was stricken with cancer that Myra realized the real importance of the hospital. She and Judy had grown up together. They had been constant friends and companions.

When Judy was diagnosed with breast cancer, Myra was devastated. Myra had been through all the same tests herself, but always with negative results. Up to this point, it was a disease that affected others. Now she understood the fear and anxiety firsthand. She had lost her husband and now faced the possibility of losing Judy.

Judy's treatment was successful, and the cancer remained in remission. Though relieved, Myra did not forget. She realized that without the hospital's medical and emotional care, others might not fare as well. This experience gave added conviction to her hospital volunteer work. She also became an active volunteer with the American Cancer Society and was involved in breast cancer awareness groups. Additionally, Myra donated $2.3 million to support local, applied research at her hospital. Myra believed that her money had little worth unless it was used to preserve the lives of others.

Myra's need to give was based on love for her friend and her desire to help others. No one needed to disparage the competition to obtain this gift. Each agency has its own constituency. The goal is to identify these individuals and demonstrate the tremendous work being done.

The Lesson

No one can create or destroy an image for another agency. Every institution stands or falls on its own merit. Focus on the agency's positive contributions and avoid comparisons.

Be a "Friend Raiser"

The Principle

Building strong relationships with important donors requires time and effort. Some of the deepest and most rewarding friendships begin in grade school, high school and college. Although friendships with donors are usually more recent, donors should be given the same special, ongoing attention as older friends. Be prepared to invest the time and energy necessary to develop and maintain these meaningful friendships.

The Story

Morgan and Joan gave $3 million to a museum in their community. As a result of that gift, their profile increased substantially. As members of the board, Morgan and Joan were well-respected among those associated with the museum. Because of their visibility, Morgan and Joan were invited to countless receptions. Bob, the museum's fund raiser, recognized and publicly acknowledged them at virtually every major event and asked the couple on occasion to give speeches about the significance of the institution to them and their part in its support.

After a year and a half of this public attention and recognition, Joan said to Morgan one day, "Don't you think that Bob is our friend only because he wants our money?" Morgan's honest response to Joan was, "That's his job, and he does it very, very well." Joan learned that fund raisers can be friends and confidential counsel just like lawyers, accountants or ministers.

Although the relationship began because of Morgan and Joan's gift, Bob built it into a strong friendship. They exchanged postcards when they went on trips. They sent notes and called one another. They gave each other interesting articles and introduced one another to like-minded friends. Bob had done his job well.

The Lesson

Many aspects of fund raising are essentially business transactions, but this does not mean that the relationships should be cold or overly formal. Just as good friendships are cultivated over time, a donor relationship should be nurtured and sustained in the same way. Think about the other person's needs and interests. Do your job and be a friend. Every successful fund raiser must also know how to be a good friend raiser.

Believe In Your Institution

The Principle

A fund raiser does not have to be a Baptist to represent a Baptist home for aging or love animals to work on behalf of the humane society, or be sports-minded to raise money for a community recreation center. It is unrealistic to expect complete resonance with all aspects of an agency. To be successful, a fund raiser *must* hold his institution in high regard.

The Story

Nina was an outstanding fund raiser. She became associated with an organization that certainly had merit, but while the cause was noble, the management lacked character. Continual salary increases, large contracts for friends and family of agency members, mismanagement, and poor oversight of the organization's finances reduced the amount of money actually used to help the clients. Nina grew more discouraged as the agency's priorities appeared to be turned upside down.

Nina finally found it necessary to resign. She no longer desired to see this particular organization receive donors' money. She did not believe in the institution.

The Lesson

Be involved with organizations that you can advance with confidence. When personal beliefs are in opposition to an agency's mission, when management or employees of an agency behave in ways that are antithetical to its own mission, or when there is doubt about an agency's ability to accomplish what is expected, do not ignore the inconsistencies. Eventually, this incongruity of belief and action will create havoc. Do not continue to tolerate a situation in which there is a serious breakdown in confidence. If it cannot be repaired, consider other options.

Honor Confidences

The Principle

Offering insider information can appear an easy way to demonstrate power, but in philanthropy, telling all you know can come back to haunt you.

The Story

Logan was a successful fund raiser with a great personality. People cared about him and appreciated everything he did for them. Over the years, Logan built a strong reputation of treating donors well. But for all his charm and talent, Logan had one conspicuous weakness—he liked to gossip. When he heard about an impending divorce, he could not wait to share the news. If he picked up information about a business setback, he quickly passed along the details. In time, people realized that telling Logan something was akin to taking out an ad in the local paper.

Jim, one of Logan's major prospects with the potential of making a gift in excess of $1 million, knew of Logan's problem. Jim decided to test Logan by offering him some personal information that was not true. The fabrication dealt with a business issue. Jim specifically asked Logan to maintain the confidence, suspecting Logan could not keep a secret.

Jim was right. Logan soon called a competitor with the news, hoping to gain a closer relationship through the offering. He pulled board members aside and passed along the story. At every opportunity, Logan used his insider information to inflate his own sense of importance.

Before long, the story got back to Jim. He called Logan and asked if they could get together. At that meeting, Jim told Logan that he had initiated the deception to see if Logan would honor his word and keep it a secret. Jim's suspicions had been confirmed. Logan could not be trusted. Jim made it clear that he would not be making any future gifts to Logan's agency.

Logan never admitted his indiscretion to anyone else. Jim, being a man of honor, chose not to divulge this incident. Logan remained with the same agency, but by failing to deal with his own shortcomings, he did not serve the agency well.

The Lesson

Handle information with discretion. Be disciplined in sharing only what is appropriate and needful. A donor relationship is valuable. Do not risk the relationship by betraying a donor's confidence. Information pandering never pays off.

Not Everyone Has to Agree

The Principle

Fund raising is not the same as trying to pass a bond issue. Everyone does not have to be consulted or in agreement. The key is to find a group of donors who have the interest and ability to financially support the work of the institution. These individuals may be a minority, but if this minority has the financial strength to insure the organization's success, things can still go forward.

The Story

A church decided to provide a child care facility that endorsed their beliefs. Those agencies supported through government programs lacked the spiritual base the church felt was needed in raising children. The cost would be $200,000 a year in operating costs, plus more than $1 million for a facility.

State-supported operations could easily bill back to the state most of the $200,000 annual cost. The capital costs would also be paid by the state over time. The elders of the church liked the money but did not like the contract.

Three of the elders searched for an appropriate facility and found a child care facility that had become vacant because the former owner, a nonprofit, could not make it work economically. They bought the building for ten percent of its cost and gave it to a new 501(c)3 that was created for the church's child care. Six other members pledged to pay $3,000 a month for 24 months to underwrite the cost of the program. Using its missionary fund, the church made up the difference.

The Lesson

Find the particular group of donors who can make the dream a reality. It is not necessary to count hands. It is what's handed that counts.

Don't Win The Christopher Columbus Award

The Principle

The Christopher Columbus Award was created to honor that adventurer who set out to find a quicker trade route to Asia, accidentally sailed into the West Indies and returned to Spain still unsure of just where he had been. In contrast, the fund raiser should set a challenging, yet obtainable goal and be systematic in achieving it.

The Story

Duane was a sculptor who believed in the art institute where he graduated, but he had never been able to make a significant gift to that institution. Richard, the president of the art institute, was a long-time fan of Duane's work. Richard continued to cultivate his relationship with Duane and watched with admiration Duane's growing success.

After a period of time, President Richard asked Duane if he would be willing to make a gift of three of his major sculptures. Those works would be used over time as a part of the institute's annual auctions. Since his notoriety was on the rise, there was a great chance that the sculptures would be auctioned for higher prices each subsequent year. This donation would represent a substantial financial gift in support of the institution. Although Duane would not be able to receive a tax deduction for the sculptures' future value, he would receive recognition at that higher level from the art institute.

The president's goals were specific: to help the institution financially and to see that Duane felt he was making an important contribution to the success of the institution. Both goals were met and over the years Duane's sculptures brought a combined total of more than $1 million to the art institute.

The Lesson

Fund-raising goals are financial, but they can also have the added benefit of advancing the relationship between a donor and the institution. Map out a realistic plan and set sail for success.

Sweat the Small Stuff

The Principle

The popular book *Don't Sweat the Small Stuff* has given people license not to worry about the details of life. While it may be good advice in some situations, in the field of philanthropy the small stuff can frequently make or break the cultivation and solicitation process.

The Story

Matilda often had questions and concerns for the children's home where she gave millions of dollars. The home consistently forgot to update her on the progress of various projects even when she asked. She was forced to read in the newspaper about a significant gift given to the home rather than receiving a call from the president. She even learned of financial mismanagement by way of the rumor mill. The whole debacle eventually came out in the news, but she still was never given any direct information. Although each issue was small on its own, collectively they convinced Matilda that while this organization did *need* her money, it did not *value* her money. Matilda chose to give to another institution that took care of the small stuff.

The Lesson

Donors notice everything. Just because they have given a large gift does not mean they have also given carte blanche. It means that they will be watching even more closely. Solicitation may be like courtship, but a strong donor relationship is like a good marriage. What mattered in the beginning—conscientious caring about all the little things—should not wane with time. Sweat the small stuff and you will not have to sweat the big stuff.

Prospects Come in All Varieties

The Principle

Look for prospects that can make a real difference in the lives of people.

The Story

Former actor Delos earmarked most of his $14 million estate for a senior citizen program in his home community. Years before, he had established a senior center in honor of his father. The majority of his estate was given in support of this work. Delos had been an actor in New York, London and Hollywood. Those who knew him were shocked that he had accumulated such wealth. He left the estate to a foundation he had established to help the elderly. Over the years, his foundation has served more than 24,000 people. Most of Delos' estate was in stocks and bonds, but more than $2 million was in property that had been purchased by his mother years ago at farm sales, sometimes for as little as 50 cents an acre.

The Lesson

Prospects are not type cast. They come in all varieties. The common denominator is ability and interest. Look beyond the preconceived notions of wealth and identify people who can make a legitimate difference in the lives of others.

Some People Are Just Waiting To Be Asked

The Principle

Every fund raiser knows she has to ask. The art of fund raising is knowing whom to ask, where to find them and when to pop the question.

The Story

"I told myself ten years ago that if anyone from the university ever found me, that I'd give them some money. Well, they found me." Malcolm, a university alum, offered this explanation regarding his lead gift to the university's Diamond Anniversary Project.

Malcolm's story is a lesson for all fund raisers. "He was literally just waiting for someone to ask him for the gift," the university's vice president said. Malcolm gave a particular type of stock that he acquired while he was president of a large corporation. The stock was worth several hundred thousand dollars and was used to buy equipment for the university department from which Malcolm graduated. "Any institution would love to have Malcolm as a supporter, and all we had to do was ask," the vice president of development added.

The Lesson

Leave no stone unturned. Do not leave prospective donors waiting to be asked.

Women Often Approach Giving Differently

The Principle

Women donors often share similar attitudes toward philanthropy. Fund raisers will benefit from better understanding their point-of-view.

The Story

Madelyn is a Des Moines philanthropist and chair of a $190 million campaign for a university. The following are Madelyn's comments regarding female philanthropists:

> "Older female philanthropists often want to stay anonymous. They may not want recognition for their gifts fearing that these gifts might seem to display bad manners, and many don't want to call on their friends to contribute. Here are some suggestions to tempt women out of their anonymity: One, select carefully a volunteer to lead the campaign—a well-liked woman willing to make a donation and step into the spotlight is the best tool for convincing other charitable women to do so. Two, offer recognition as a gift to future women. I commonly ask women who don't want their gifts acknowledged, 'When was the last time you saw a woman's name on a building?' A woman's name on a plaque always allows future generations to know that women have

contributed. Three, emphasize the greater good. I point out that when women call on peers for donations, the money is not always for themselves. Women must focus on the organization and the good their contributions will do. Four, educate on the pleasure of giving. Stress that giving time and energy to a worthwhile organization can be great fun."

The Lesson

Encourage, but do not force women to enjoy the benefits of philanthropy. They may not be initially inclined to see recognition as an appropriate aspect of giving, but take measures to see that they do not miss out on receiving honor where it's due.

What To Be... (Or Not To Be)

The Principle

Volunteers are the lifeblood of any organization. Here are a few tips for motivating volunteer staff, increasing productivity and reducing turnover.

1. **Good management.** Be organized. Offer appreciation. Treat them like customers. Give them positive experiences.
2. **Make it meaningful.** Don't take them for granted. Respect their time. Keep them busy. Don't let them wait for something to do.
3. **Promote from within.** As in the corporate world, the possibility of promotion encourages hard work. Give them more responsibility.
4. **Offer training.** Send them to workshops. Spend time training them yourself. Show them you're committed to them. You've given them a great experience if they can learn and improve their skills while making a difference in your organization.
5. **Make room for them to grow.** Make it clear that there is room for everyone to move up in the ranks—from letter stuffer to administrative assistant, from administrative assistant to event organizer or publicist. If your volunteer wants a chance to move up, make it happen.
6. **Know your volunteers personally.** Don't make them feel like a number. Remember that they are volunteering their most valuable possession—their time.

The Lesson

A leading Kansas City philanthropist and volunteer offered her advice on how to deal with major donors.

1. **Be involved.** Prospective donors want to know that you have already given your gift. Your donation says that your money is where your mouth is.

2. **Be excited.** Your enthusiasm will come through in your presentation and is certain to be contagious.

3. **Be confident.** Your confidence will instill faith in your prospect who will be much more likely to give to your cause.

4. **Be sincere.** If you sincerely believe in your organization's mission, your earnestness will be obvious to your prospect.

5. **Be prepared.** Be armed with the right information. Prospects will expect to see an organization's financial statements, annual reports and strategic plan.

6. **Be positive.** Don't mention negative issues or problems within your organization unless you feel that they need to be addressed in order to be more credible.

7. **Be professional.** You may know your prospects socially, but treat the appointment as a business call. Get straight to the point. Be articulate. Express clearly your organization's mission and how the donor's gift will help.

8. **Be candid.** Clearly articulate what you expect from the donor. Not asking up front for a specific amount may result in a smaller gift.

9. **Be open.** Perhaps the prospect has ideas on how the gift would be best used. The gift must mean something to the donor so it's important to let the donor have a sense of ownership.

10. **Be appreciative.** No matter what size the gift, show the donor that you appreciate the contribution. If the prospect turns you down for your gift, show that you appreciate their time.

Just
The
Beginning

Strategies one to 100 are not simply formulas to be followed. Rather, they represent a philosophy of fund raising that is meant to be lived out naturally. This philosophy cannot be worn externally as an overcoat; it needs to be internalized. By only going through the motions of each strategy, limited success may be achieved, but to experience consistent, growing success, the philosophy of fund raising presented through the many principles, stories, and lessons in this book must start inside and work their way out. It may take a second reading, it may take some quiet pondering and it may take some honest soul-searching to really take hold of the heartbeat of the message.

What is the message? Fund raising is not about sales; it is about service. Fund raising is not an occupation, it is an opportunity to serve. Fund raising is not a chance to be somebody special; it is a chance to do something important. It is not about self; it is about improving lives.

If the focus is on achieving success, recognition and reward, a fund raiser will often fall short of his expectations. But by striving to achieve success and recognition for others, a fund raiser will often experience reward far beyond her expectations.

I hope that this book will help to advance philanthropy as a whole and benefit fund raisers, donors, workers, volunteers and those served by their institutions. Money is practically limitless. Need is practically limitless. What is limited are the people with the heart to help make the right connections. Today would be a good day to get started. Today would be a good day to raise a million dollars and have a donor thank you.

About
The
Author

Bob Hartsook, author, speaker and consultant, has influenced the direction of philanthropy. His thoughts and experiences have helped both the novice and the experienced fund raiser in closing gifts of a million dollars or more.

Speaking to thousands of professionals and volunteers, he focuses on the demands of raising funds today. His trademarked Integrated Fund-Raising Campaign has helped countless institutions achieve maximum financial goals exceeding billions of dollars. On the pages of the most popular fund-raising journals, magazines and newsletters, including *Fund Raising Management, NSFRE News, Chronicle of Philanthropy, Planned Giving Today, NonProfit Times* and many others, he articulates the significant challenges facing fund raisers.

In 1998, Dr. Hartsook's first book, *Closing that Gift! How to be Successful 99% of the Time*, was received enthusiastically. This second book on million-dollar gifts gives Dr. Hartsook the opportunity to tell the stories that have been delighting audiences for years.

His consulting firms, Hartsook and Associates and Essential Philanthropic Services, have conducted hundreds of campaigns and regularly maintain a diverse national client list.

Prior to starting Hartsook and Associates in 1987, Dr. Hartsook served as Executive Vice President of the Kansas Engineering Society and as Vice President of Colby Community College, Washburn University and Wichita State University. At Wichita State he was named president of the Board of Trustees. Dr. Hartsook holds a Bachelor of Arts

Degree in Economics, a Master of Science in Counseling, a Juris Doctor and a Doctor of Education Degree.

Bob Hartsook lives with his son, Austin, in Wilmington, North Carolina.

You may contact Dr. Hartsook at:

Dr. Robert F. Hartsook, President
Hartsook and Associates
1501 Castle Rock
Wichita, KS 67230
Telephone 316.733.7100
Facsimile 316.733.7103
E-mail rhartsook@aol.com
www.HartsookGroup.com

ASR
Philanthropic
Publishing

ASR Philanthropic Publishing serves the fund-raising and philanthropic community with a variety of publications designed to inform and educate, as well as stimulate thought and discussion by professionals throughout the United States.

ASR publications include newsletters, books and monographs, as well as audio and video products.

ASR's Reference Collection monographs and books may be purchased in small or large quantities. Discounts apply to large-quantity orders.

For large-quantity monograph orders, ASR can imprint your organization's logo or trademark on each copy.

ASR customizes and binds collections of monographs that meet your organization's reference needs.

ASR Philanthropic Publishing has an active custom-publishing division that creates books, newsletters, brochures and other print material for use by fund-raising and philanthropic organizations. We are available to consult on your organization's specific needs.

To order or receive information about any of ASR's publications or programs please contact:

ASR Philanthropic Publishing
P.O. Box 782648
Wichita, Kansas 67278
Telephone 316.733.7470
Facsimile 316.733.7103

ASR Philanthropic Publishing Reference Collection Monograph's

From prospect research through donor recognition, ASR's Reference Collection Monographs address the important topics in fund raising and philanthropic management today. Written by leading experts, including Robert F. Hartsook and Arthur C. Frantzreb, these to-the-point publications are essential tools for fund raisers who excel. Here is a current list of available Reference Collection Monographs.

ANNUAL GIVING

#01-001   It's Worth a $5 Million Endowment

#01-002   Insuring the Annual Fund Program of Non-Profit Organizations. Announcing: The Forward Fund

CAPITAL CAMPAIGNS

#02-001   10 Impediments to Campaign Success

#02-002   Why You Don't Need the 800-Pound Gorilla

#02-003   Stick to the Basics

#02-004   What to Do When The Campaign Is Over

#02-005   Identifying the Significant Gift Opportunity

#02-006   The Sizzle Factor

#02-007   30 Commandments for Successful Fund Raising

#02-008   Chanute Depot Restoration Project: If at First You Don't Succeed …

#02-009   Campaign For Dignity: Cerebral Palsy Research Foundation

#02-010   The Secret of Campaign Success: How Kansas Special Olympics Raised $1.35 Million

#02-011   Great Empires Aren't Built in a Day: Magic Empire Council of Girl Scouts

#02-012   Strength Amidst Change: St. Luke's Hospital Foundation

#02-013   Feasibility Studies: Probability? or Productivity!

#02-014   Inter-Faith Ministries: Fund-Raising Fears No More

ENDOWMENT

#05-001   Endowment Fund Raising Made Easy

#03-002   You Can Get an Endowment

#03-003   Endowment: What is it? How does it work?

GRANTWRITING

#04-001   Foundations Are Human, Too

#04-002   The ABCs of Grantwriting, or Always Be Certain

#04-003   Essential Tips on Securing Governmental Grants

PHILANTHROPIC MANAGEMENT

PLANNED GIVING

PROSPECT RESEARCH

RECOGNITION

SOLICITATION

CULTIVATION

BOARD DEVELOPMENT

VOLUNTEERS

MAJOR GIFTS

To order a Monograph of The Resource Collection please call 1.877.7GIVING.